HUMAN
EMPOWERMENT
TOWARDS
PEACE

HUMAN EMPOWERMENT TOWARDS PEACE

The Works of One Man

ASSOC. PROF. J. O. ENEH PH.D.

authorHOUSE®

AuthorHouse™
1663 Liberty Drive
Bloomington, IN 47403
www.authorhouse.com
Phone: 1 (800) 839-8640

Published by AuthorHouse 05/04/2015

ISBN: 978-1-5049-0791-0 (sc)
ISBN: 978-1-5049-0790-3 (e)

Print information available on the last page.

Any people depicted in stock imagery provided by Thinkstock are models, and such images are being used for illustrative purposes only. Certain stock imagery © Thinkstock.

This book is printed on acid-free paper.

CONTENTS

INTRODUCTION 1

CHAPTER ONE: CAUSES OF WAR.. 5

1.1   Causes of War in our Modern Time 7
       Ignorance/ Lack of Education 7
       Poverty/ Lack of Human Empowerment 8
       Injustice 9
       Quest for supremacy 10
1.2   World War I and Its Effects on World Peace..............12
1.3.   World War II and its Effects on World Peace.............13
1.4   Efforts to Forestall Further Occurrence of World War 14

CHAPTER TWO: REVIEW OF SOME LITERATURE ON
               PEACE MODEL 16

2.1.   What is the Peace Model?...............................16
2.2.   Mahatma Gandhi's Peace Model...........................16
2.3.   Nelson Mandela's Model of Peace........................17
2.4.   Stephen Richards Covey's Peace Model...................18

CHAPTER THREE: EDEH'S CHARITY/ *MMADI* PEACE
                 MODEL 20

3.1.   Edeh's MMADI Peace Model 20
3.2.   The Individual Tranquillity as a Basic Constituent of Edeh's
       Charity Peace Model 22
3.3.   Edeh's Intra-and Inter-Religious Peace Initiatives.............25
3.4.   Edeh's Intra-and Inter Cultural Peace Initiatives 27
3.5.   The International Effects of Fr Edeh's Peace Initiatives 28
3.6.   Practical Application Of Edeh's Charity/MMADI Peace
       Model 29

3.7.   The Centre for Peace, Justice and Reconciliation, Elele ...31

3.8.   Characteristics of Edeh's Peace Model.............................34

         The Situation of 'No Victor No Vanquished'...................34

         Recovery of Everlasting Peace 35

3.9.   Practical Results of Edeh's Charity Peace Model 36

a.   In the Area of Business 36

b.   A Land Case between the Mgbalukwu-isu and Ogboji-Ezzagu Communities in Ebonyi State.............................38

c.   A Land Dispute between Ugbene and Ugbenu in Anambra State 40

CHAPTER FOUR: EDUCATIONAL/ ECONOMIC EMPOWERMENT OF THE YOUTH AND SOCIETAL STABILITY............... 41

Concept of Empowerment and Poverty Alleviation 42

Educational Empowerment 43

4.1.   Some Fundamental Facts about Education in Nigeria 43

4.2.   The Government Takeover of Missionary Schools and Its Effects 44

4.3.   The Outcome of The School "Take–Over" by The Nigerian Government 45

4.4.   The Quest to Establish the First Polytechnic and College of Education in Nigeria 46

4.5.   The Quest to Establish the First Private University in West Africa 48

4.6.   Edeh's Role in Nigeria's Educational Sector....................50

         Educational Empowerment...51

         Socio-Economic Empowerment 53

4.7.   Edeh's Education for All 53

         Special Features of Edeh's Educational Empowerment.....54

4.8.   Economic Empowerment through the Creation of Job Opportunities 56

4.9.   Edeh's Employed Workers Chart (EEWC)......................57

4.10. The Unique nature of Edeh's economic empowerment....58

CHAPTER FIVE: MADONNA INTERNATIONAL CHARITY PEACE AWARD 60

5.1. The Meaning and Purpose 60
5.2 The Origin of the Madonna International Charity Peace Award...61
5.3. Who is Eligible to Win the Award?................................62
5.4. The Journey so far................................63
5.5. The Relevance of MICPA to our Modern World............64

CHAPTER SIX: RELIGIOUS INSTITUTIONS AS MEANS OF PERPETUATING PEACE 66

6.1. Religion..66
6.2. Institutions (Congregations)................................68
6.3. Edeh's Religious Institutions as an Agent of Peace............69
6.4. Religious Institutions 70
a. The Sisters of Jesus the Saviour (SJS) 70
b. The Fathers of Jesus the Saviour (FJS) 70
c. The Contemplatives of Jesus the Saviour (Male) 72
d. The Contemplatives of Jesus the Saviour (Female)..........72
e. The Catholic Prayer Ministry (CPM) 73
f. The Pilgrimage Centre of Eucharistic Adoration, Elele, Nigeria 73

CONCLUSION.. 77

BIBLIOGRAPHY 81

INTRODUCTION

Ontologically man is a creature that desires peace. This explains why, despite innumerable abortive attempts to achieve it, it has continued to receive the best of attentions both in local and international communities. The reason behind this is not farfetched. It is an indisputable fact that peace remains the pillar that supports and sustains every other thing desired by man. Without peace you cannot talk of security, without peace every talk on development will remain a figment of imagination, without peace advancement in any field of study cannot be actualized (Melladu, 2013, p.12).

Ironically, this most important value upon which the success of man depends is the most elusive of all that humanity longs for especially in the contemporary society characterized by unbridled terror, mutual economic and political exploitation of the less privileged by the strong, gender discrimination, religious fanaticism, racism, class inequality etc. Consequently, the cosmos has consistently continued to be chaotic as a result of the aforementioned untamed barbarism and hostility often unleashed on man by man. In the past, these gave birth to all the inhuman events in the history of mankind such as slave trade and slavery, colonialism, apathy, the Holocaust, etc. (Kaitus, 1998, p.128).

After the abolition of slavery and gradual obliteration of colonialism, it has taken much time and resources to reinstate authentic peace between the enslaved, the colonized, and their masters. The fact that it has not been achieved explains why Africa has continued to blame her backwardness on the West leading to a relationship of constant suspicion.

Apart from economic and socio-political factors, more than a few have argued, and persuasively too, that illiteracy is responsible for the high rate of unlawfulness in our world today, but if this position is dragged to the judgement seat of critical analysis, it will not hold water because our universities and other tertiary institutions are turning out graduates in the thousands on yearly basis. The question then is: why is peace still eluding us amidst the current level of literacy in the world? This goes a long way to show that our education lacks its substance. It is against this background that Fr Edeh sets out to give to the youths of our time a holistic education that leaves the educated a brushed gentleman or woman that sues for development, progress, and peaceful co-existence in the human community. This is an education that takes cognisance of the ideal identity of man as a being created in the image of God who is all good and as such needs maximum protection, peace, and love.

Consequently, in all Edeh's institutions, ranging from primary to tertiary, education is not only about the transmission of skills necessary for gainful employment through the practice of a trade or profession but morality and spirituality—the basic things that differentiate us from beasts—are taken very seriously as well. Accordingly, all the students here are committed to obtaining the kind of education and training that will allow them to develop their talents and abilities in such a way that each one will be able to make a contribution to their family, community, nation, and the world as a whole (The Saviourite Magazine, 2012/2013, p. 15).

For Edeh, education goes beyond instructions received in the class room—it consists of the total environment in which a person lives, the family unit, the peer group, and the society at large, so all these are put into consideration while the students undergo their training. The family, as the foundation of society, plays an important role in teaching young people moral and spiritual values. Just like parents, Edeh compels all the teachers and lecturers to set the examples for their young students to see and copy. Values such as living together with people of different cultures and creed, cooperation with one another, and esteem for all members of humanity are usually emphasized in all Edeh's institutions so as to educate the youths for a peaceful society.

Students from these institutions represent different races, cultures, religions, and social/economic strata of our society gathered together for a common goal. Their diversity is symbolic of their belief in the oneness of mankind and the elimination of all forms of prejudice and bias against each other. Their goal is the harmony of different people working in cooperation towards a common goal—peace.

This peaceful coexistence of students from different nationalities under Fr Edeh's tutelage is an illustration of the rich diversity of humanity and the good in nourishing those cultural differences that bring us together. Respect for each other's views and an understanding of the common humanity we share through the realization that we are all a divine creation connected by indissoluble bonds—this is essentially what matters. This is at the basis of the motivation and action of this great African thinker to resolve the crucial social and economic problems facing humanity.

Quite aware of the dualistic nature of man (body and soul), Edeh therefore in all his universities and other tertiary institutions, advocates for a well-oriented high-quality university education that is aimed at preparing the students for a fruitful life here on Earth and a glorified life in heaven. The institutions take, as their priority, a sound moral and ethical education that directs the conscience of the students towards behaving well and avoiding evil, towards a wholesome love of God and their neighbour. In these institutions, the emphasis placed on academic excellence is the same amount of accent placed on character formation and good moral conduct.

Consequently, candidates come as youths with shrouded visions and graduate as well-formed citizens properly equipped to go out and wage war against the ills that bedevil our world and hinder the possibility of peaceful coexistence among individuals, families, organizations, and nations.

As a result, it has been on record that graduates from all Fr Edeh's institutions do, through the influence of Edeh, constitute themselves into ambassadors of peace wherever they discover themselves. This, as a matter of fact, distinguishes Edeh as a pillar of education in Africa as no one else in this continent has had the opportunity of directly influencing such number of youths as he does. Through the proper holistic education of thousands of the youths who are privileged to pass through Edeh's numerous educational institutions, the youth are highly empowered, thus peace is highly engendered into the lives, the families, and communities of millions of people in this world.

CHAPTER ONE

CAUSES OF WAR

It is a fact that peace is lacking in today's world. Man is constantly inundated by factors that delimit both his outer and inner peace. But just as Raimon Panikkar observes: "It is difficult to live without outer peace; it is impossible to live without inner peace" (Panikkar, in Kunnumpuram, 2007, p. 159). In the light of this, the search for peace becomes of immense importance.

In the prehistoric era, by means of myths which have been identified as the language of the prehistoric people, war was identified as present before the creation of the world and even instrumental to the forging of the universe. Similarly, in the historic era, philosophers seemed to corroborate this view asserting or implying that war has been instrumental and indeed necessary in the evolvement of the universe. The import of these claims is that the cause of war is nature itself. In other words, war is intrinsic in the nature of the world.

Very similar to the above view is that of Heraclitus (540-480 BC), an ancient philosopher from Ephesus better known for his 'flux theory'. His view was that all things are constantly changing. He posited that at the heart of this change is strife. "For him, strife is the very essence of change itself. The conflict of opposites that we see in the world is not a calamity, but is simply the permanent condition of all things" (Stumpf and Fieser, 2003, p. 17). Thus, in Heraclitus' submission, conflict is a necessary constituent of the universe.

Going down the same ladder, Hobbes, an English modern philosopher, in his major philosophical work *The Leviathan,* paints a picture of a state of nature (i.e. the earliest condition of human existence before the formation of civil society with its attendant governments) that is replete with conflict and wars. He posits that it is the state of utter chaos, characterized by egoistic quest, dominated by a concupisciable element and struggle for power, glory, and security. Hobbes styled the existential condition at that time as "the war of all against all" (Stumpf and Fieser, 2003, p. 217). In that state of nature, there was a perpetual state of unrest, continual and unmitigated suspicion, unavoidable fear of violence and death, etc. Hobbes summed it as follows:

> "In such condition, there is no place for industry because the fruit thereof is uncertain: and consequently no culture of the earth ... no knowledge of the face of the earth, no account of time; no arts; no letters; no society; and which is worse of all, continual fear, and danger of violent death and the life of man is solitary, poor, nasty, brutish and short" (Hobbes, Thomas, Leviathan, p.17).

Taking a position very similar to that of Heraclitus as stated above, Karl Marx, a contemporary German philosopher, asserts in the preface of his major philosophical work as follows:

> "The history of all hitherto existing society is the history of class struggles, freeman and slave... oppressor and oppressed stood in constant opposition to one another, carried on an uninterrupted, now hidden, now open fight, a fight that each time ended either in a revolutionary reconstruction of society at large, or in the common mind of the contending classes (Karl Marx and Engels, 1962, pp. 1, 362).

Going by the above exposition, one may see war as simply a necessity for existence and as predating the human society.

As the saying goes, violence begets violence. Consequently, a change birthed by violent revolution would be ousted by another violent revolution. Our principal assumption in this work therefore is that social change can be achieved without violence and wars and that a change wrought through this means is better founded.

1.1   CAUSES OF WAR IN OUR MODERN TIME

War here is understood in the widest sense of the term: the absence of peace. Peace, as noted earlier, has two dimensions, namely the inner peace (peace within) and the outer peace (peace without). The absence of peace in any of these dimensions entails unimaginable terror to mankind. A holistic approach, therefore, is necessary if a satisfactory panacea is ever to be achieved. Consequent upon this, the causes of war we shall discuss will include factors that delimit both peace within and peace without. It is important to note that any factor that delimits peace is considered as a cause of war. A number of factors could be identified as causes of wars. They include ignorance, poverty, injustice, oppression, conflict of interest, power tussle, etc. We shall examine them one after another.

Ignorance/ Lack of Education

It is an observable fact that the spitefulness of war in recent times is less than it was in earlier times in history when war and empire building were the aspiration of most, if not every, monarch. Such names as Napoleon, Alexander the Great and many more were venerated for their war escapades. Today such names as Mahatma Gandhi, Martin Luther King Jr., Nelson Mandela, Emmanuel, M.P. Edeh, etc. are venerated for their campaign against war.

A number of things are responsible for this change in attitude; prominent among them are increase in enlightenment and a better educational system.

Good education, no doubt, is an antidote to barbaric acts such as violence and war. According to Herbert Spencer, the object of education is the formation of character (Okafor, F., 2006, p. 18). Similarly, R.M. Hutchins asserts that the "aim of formal education should be to develop that faculty which sets man apart from the other animals" (Okafor, F., 2006, p. 127). The animal-like untrained, uneducated nature in us is that which generates the chaos which the Hobbesian state of nature decries. Thus, education prunes away this animal-like nature in humans, developing that faculty which makes him uniquely human.

A good cultivated reason (which is the function of education) decries the unwarranted murder and maiming of other human beings which are usually the result of war. Persons therefore who are well educated would always be on the side of peace.

However, it is to be noted that education entails the transfer of knowledge, belief, or culture from one person to another. There is formal and informal education. From this point of view, it can be argued that education can be a source of increasing violence since a person who is vitiated or a religious group which believes that killing those who do not belong to their group is God's will can transfer such belief to others resulting in increased unrest and violence.

It could also be argued that education can jeopardize peace. The increase in the volume and quality of knowledge today has made the production of sophisticated weapons of mass destruction possible to the point of endangering the human race should any other major global war breaks out.

This highlights the importance of good education, for surely, it is not every transfer of knowledge, belief, and culture that promotes peace, but the transfer of good knowledge, belief, and culture. Any culture or system of belief that is incongruent with reason especially as regards man's happiness, security, and progress should be regulated from being transferred. This immediately brings to mind the importance of the agent of education.

Thus, the question is not just attending a school and being educated, but which type of school does one attend and what sort of education is being inculcated into the students of that school? Edeh's schools and how they inculcate good education and morals come into play as we shall see in subsequent chapters.

Poverty/ Lack of Human Empowerment

A popular saying that "a hungry man is an angry man" restates an age-long experience. Poverty begins with destabilizing the inner peace of individuals and then goes on to destabilize the peace of the society at large. Can you imagine what it is like to be hungry and unable to afford a decent meal; to have children and not have the wherewithal to train them in school; to be without a shelter and or clothing—abandoned to the hazards of nature; to be lampooned, lambasted, rejected, derided, and cajoled because you belong to the class of the anawims in the society; to watch a loved one die because the hospital bill could not be afforded, etc.? Sure, such phenomena elicit anger, worries, depression, and even suicide. These are veritable signs of inner conflict (deficiency in peace within).

Envision for instance a room filled to capacity by people who are angry. The tension in such an environment would be better imagined than experienced. The slightest provocation which otherwise would have elicited laughter or at list no negative reaction could trigger a bitter conflict. Similarly, any society populated by angry citizens must be a very volatile society.

Poverty could be caused either by a person's inability to work for his daily bread due to natural deformity, or by a person's inability to work because he lacks the formal training- education, or a person's inability to work because he is physically able and formally educated but there is no employment opportunity for him. We shall see later in this book how Edeh empowers all these categories of people.

An idle mind, it is said, is the devil's workshop. A person who is idle due to lack of job is more susceptible to taking to arms and disrupting the peace of the society. At this point, lack of human empowerment has moved from the disruption of the inner peace of the individual to the disruption of the peace of the community. Such a person can be easily enticed into joining a group that has as its occupation the disruption of societal peace, such as organized terror groups, bands of armed robbers, kidnappers, etc. Contrarily, when one is empowered to take care of one's daily needs, one would possess the inner peace and would be less prone to disrupt the peace of the society.

Injustice

Injustice is an eclectic concept. That is, it can be understood in different ways. "In philosophy and jurisprudence, the dominant view has been that injustice and justice are two sides of the same coin—that injustice is simply a lack of justice" (Wikipedia, 2014). Some, however, such as Judith Shklar, Thomas W. Simon, and Eric Heinze have argued that justice and injustice are independent qualities.

Injustice entails every kind of sectarian thinking or attitude: tribalism, nepotism, sexism, chauvinism, favouritism, etc. It is a close ally to the famous expression: group benevolence and outside group malevolence. It involves treating some persons or group with undue favour at the expense of others; often to the point of marginalizing or discriminating or oppressing them.

Injustice has been a major cause of wars in the world history. Dr. Martin Luther King Jr. once asserted, "Injustice anywhere is a threat to justice everywhere" (Martin Luther King Jr., Letter from a Birmingham Jail, 1963). "The sense of injustice can be a powerful motivational condition, causing people to take action not just to defend themselves but also others who they perceive to be unfairly treated" (Wikipedia, 2014). This is evident in the history of many nations and indeed the history of the world.

In Nigeria for instance, the civil war or the Nigerian-Biafran War was the child of a perceived injustice. The Niger-Delta Crisis also has the imprint of injustice as its root cause. In other parts of the world, the Hutu-Tutsi War in Rwanda, the French Revolution, the English Revolution, the Irish revolution, the American Civil war and indeed most of the wars and conflicts witnessed in the world history have some connection with injustice.

Quest for supremacy

Nobody ever wants to be relegated to the background. The craving to be on top seems to be an innate instinct in man. Over the years, this tendency has resulted in many bitter experiences. Nevertheless, in itself, guided by good and informed reason, this instinct (tendency to be on top) can yield a good result. It can be the base of a healthy competition which derives the wheel of development forward. It is this competiveness that makes sports intriguing. This competitiveness in educational sector makes for academic excellence. In science and technology, this competiveness engenders landmark breakthroughs, innovations, and mouth-watering discoveries that are capable of improving man's condition.

Contrarily, when this same sense of competitiveness is not guided by good and educated (informed) reason, it creates and propels disharmony, conflict and wars, robbing man of both his inner and outer peace. In the primitive era, it is this competitiveness that drove the empires into wars which were prevalent at that time. This competitiveness was majorly the cause of inter tribal wars that made life and progress impossible in some sense. It is this quest for superiority or the claim of superiority that gave impetus to what has been described as the scramble for Africa—colonialism.

In the present, this quest for superiority still engenders what is known in some quarters as neo-colonialism. It is this quest for superiority that propels the armament race that has been, and at the present in a more conspicuous manner, the bane of world peace. It is this armament race and the quest to curtail it (cognizant of the dangers it harbors) that have been the cause of the rift between United States of America and some other countries like Iran, Syria, Japan, etc.

The truth is that nobody, no nation or their military wants to feel inferior. The more sophisticated weapon of mass destruction you have, the more powerful you will feel. Thus, these nations spend huge sums of their resources on acquiring and developing weapons of mass destruction. Between 1908 and 1913 for instance, the military spending of the European powers increased by 50% (Prior, 1999, p. 18). One intrigue in this is that, when a country feels that it has acquired very large quantity and quality weapons, it would (unconsciously and even sometimes consciously) begin to make moves that are capable of bridging peace. It would sometimes long for opportunity to showcase its military might—for what is the need of spending so much on ammunition when it is never used?

It is pertinent to note that some of these causes do not act in isolation. Sometimes a number of causes are required to bring about war. Let us examine the major wars in the world history namely, World War I and World War II to ascertain the verity of this claim.

1.2   WORLD WAR I AND ITS EFFECTS ON WORLD PEACE

World War I, or the First World War as some might like to call it, was a war that engulfed almost the whole globe, though it was centered in Europe. The war began on 28 July 1914 and lasted until 11 November 1918, involving about 65 million men of which over 10 million were killed and more than 20 million wounded. In the 1900s, Europe was divided into two major coalitions: the Central Powers and the Allied Powers. The Allied Powers included the United Kingdom, France, Belgium, Serbia, Montenegro, and the Russian Empire (Keylor, William R., Microsoft Encarta, 2009). The Central Powers, on the other hand consisted of the empires of Germany and Austria-Hungary. These coalitions were formed with view of being invincible should any war break out.

The immediate cause of the war was the murder of Archduke Francis Ferdinand, the heir to the throne of Austria-Hungary, by a Serbian nationalist Gavrilo Princip at Serajevo (Keylor, William R., Microsoft Encarta, 2009). Diplomatic crisis soon followed. Austria-Hungary delivered an ultimatum (which Serbia could not meet) to the Kingdom of Serbia (Taylor, 1998, pp. 8093; Djokiæ, 2003, p. 24). The International alliances were invoked and soon the major powers were at war. As the war proceeded, it continued to web in other nations within and outside of Europe.

The war finally came to an end on 11 November 1918 with the defeat of the Central Powers. The effect of this defeat was enormous. The political order of Europe was greatly transformed; The German, Austro-Hungarian, Russian, and Ottoman empires collapsed and new areas were carved out of their former lands. Further, the boundaries of many other countries were redrawn. The war also helped precipitate the Bolshevik Revolution in Russia (Keylor, William R., Microsoft Encarta, 2009).

The war also had important long-term consequences. The enormous cost of the war undermined the financial stability of all the countries involved, and they had to bear an onerous burden of debt for many years to come. These financial losses, combined with the battlefield deaths and physical destruction, severely weakened the European powers (Keylor, William R., Microsoft Encarta, 2009).

1.3. WORLD WAR II AND ITS EFFECTS ON WORLD PEACE

The First World War ended, leaving Germany weak and disadvantaged. The Germans were forced to sign the Treaty of Versailles at their own disadvantage. First, the Germans were deprived of some portions of its pre-war territory, such as Alsace and Lorraine, the city of Danzig (Gdańsk), and the Polish Corridor. Second, Germany was unilaterally disarmed and forced to accept an Allied military occupation of the Rhineland and to give up its colonial empire. Third, Germany was forced to accept the responsibility for the outbreak of the war and was required to pay the cost of repairing the wartime damage, known as reparations (Keylor, William R., Microsoft Encarta, 2009). This left the Germans with some sense of marginalization.

In the face of this, Hitler emerged promising to "overturn the Versailles Treaty and secure additional Lebensraum (living space) for the German people, who he contended deserved more as members of a superior race" (Keylor, William R., Microsoft Encarta, 2009). The depression that hit Germany in the early 1930s and the failure of the moderate parties to properly address it led many voters to turn to the Nazis and the Communists. Consequently, in 1933, Hitler became the German Chancellor, and in time, established himself as a dictator.

True to his promise, Hitler reintroduced conscription and created a new air force. He also produced new weapons which he tried out on the side of right-wing military rebels in the Spanish Civil War (1936-1939). Between 1936 and 1940, Germany, Italy, and Japan signed treaties that created a coalition between them. Still keeping to his promise, Hitler began his expansionist campaign. He first annexed Austria in March

1938, soon Czechoslovakia followed in March 1939, next was Poland. The Soviet Union, which had signed a pact not to enter into war with Germany, also invaded Poland and then Finland. The war continued to web in more countries like Britain, France, Japan, America and indeed most parts of the world, including the colonies belonging to the major European countries.

The Second World War which began in 1939 eventually came to an end in 1945 with the defeat of Germany, Japan, and Italy—the axis. The Allies could claim the victory, but the cost on both sides was enormous. The United States, for instance, spent an estimated $341 billion on the war. Germany spent $272 billion, the Soviet Union $192 billion; Britain $120 billion; Italy $94 billion; Japan $56 billion, etc. (Ziemke, Earl F., Microsoft Encarta, 2009). However, with the exception of the United States, the money spent on the war cannot equate the war's true cost. The USSR is estimated to have lost 30 percent of its national wealth. Similarly the full economic cost of the war to Japan has been estimated at $562 billion.

The human losses of the war are even more disheartening. "Most experts estimate the military and civilian losses of Allied forces at 44 million and those of the Axis at 11 million" (Ziemke, Earl F., Microsoft Encarta, 2009). Whenever World War II is mentioned, such ugly incidents like the Holocaust that claimed about 6 million Jews, the bombing of Hiroshima and Nagasaki which claimed innumerable lives and disfigured so many generations stare us in the face.

1.4 EFFORTS TO FORESTALL FURTHER OCCURRENCE OF WORLD WAR

At the end of the First World War, the world was appalled by the level of cruelty it amounted to. People longed that such occurrence never repeat itself in history. This was the concern of most countries that witnessed the war. The means of achieving this, it was conceived, was to "create an international body whose sole purpose was to maintain world peace and which would sort out international disputes as and when they occurred" (Chris Trueman, 2013), thus the League of Nations came into existence.

The League of Nations was to first call the disputing countries to dialogue (should any dispute ensue between nations) and decide on a way forward. It was to verbally sanction the aggressive nation and, if it fails to retrace its steps, economic sanction was to follow, and when these fail, military might be employed to force the aggressor to retrace its steps. However, the League of Nations never had at its disposal any military force. The countries that would have supplied the military force were adversely weakened by the First World War. Consequently, the League could not keep the peace it was created to preserve. The outbreak of the Second World War is an eloquent testimony of this.

The world did not give up its quest for peace and security. Once again an international body was formed to replace the League of Nations. It was at the instigation of Franklin D. Roosevelt, the then U.S. president, that the United Nations (U.N.) was called. This was said to have officially taken off on 25 June 1945 (Chris Trueman, 2013) with 50 member countries who signed the charter at San Francisco on the above date. The member countries were to contribute to build the military power of the association hence, the weakness that crippled the League of Nations was taken care of.

Nevertheless, the question still remains: has the United Nations succeeded in bringing about world peace? Current experiences convince us that it has not succeeded. One must acknowledge that some feat has been achieved. But if truth must be said, the much desired world peace is still farfetched. So many theories, so many ideologies have been propounded by Desmond Tutu, Nelson Mandela, Mahatma Gandhi, Steve Cove, Emmanuel Edeh, etc. promising to bring peace to the heart of man. Among these theories and ideologies, Edeh's Peace Models shine brightest.

CHAPTER TWO

REVIEW OF SOME LITERATURE ON PEACE MODEL

2.1. WHAT IS THE PEACE MODEL?

Over the years, humanity has laboured under local, regional, and international tension. Being a comfort and tranquility-seeking being, man loathes violence. The proliferation of violence, the burden of depression and despair around the world call urgently for peace. In every epoch, the human family has had peace crusaders—men and women of exceptional ingenuity who, theoretically and pragmatically, have strenuously laboured to bring about peace to the human family. In their labours, many have evolved ingenious peace models that have impacted tremendously on the community of humans.

A peace model therefore is an operational principle or policies that could be applied or followed in attaining peace. Thus, it is pertinent to briefly expose some of these globally outstanding peace models.

2.2. MAHATMA GANDHI'S PEACE MODEL

Besides his religious inclination, hostile and inhuman treatments that confronted Gandhi on arrival in South Africa were the immediate influences to his struggle for peace among people. On his arrival in South Africa on May 1893, he experienced the effect of hostile and inhuman legislations –whites against the Indian community. Relating Gandhi's own personal humiliation on arrival, Enuga S. Reddy (former Assistant Secretary of the United Nations) explained: "Travelling to Pretoria soon after his arrival in Durban, he was thrown off a train, assaulted by a coachman and denied a hotel room in Johannesburg—all because of his colour."

To fight the unjust laws and inhuman treatments meted on the Indians, Gandhi started with the establishment of the National Indian Congress and the Transvaal British Indian Association to make representations to the authorities. With such organisations, Gandhi aimed at engaging the authorities in dialogue for a possible abrogation of legislations that disenfranchised a few Indians who had qualified, legislation that refused trading licenses to Indians, the imposed and obnoxious "three-pound tax" on all "free Indians," and in Transvaal, the most dehumanizing ordinance requiring all Indians to register with ten fingerprints and to show the registration certificates whenever demanded by the police.

These dehumanizing legislations constituted the driving force of Gandhi's Peace Model. He consequently developed principles that would guide the marginalized Indians in their quest for peace. The principles were embedded in two strong values, namely: the values of love-force or non-violence (Ahimsa) and its practical application (Satyagraha). By these principles, they were to sue for peace and actualize their integral emancipation through non-violent and love-driven mental and physical activities. These principles and their alignments formed the central tenets of Gandhi's Peace Model.

2.3. NELSON MANDELA'S MODEL OF PEACE

Nelson Madiba Mandela

Being a member of the higher echelon of the opposition party—ANC—against the oppressing party—National Party, he was arrested, imprisoned, and released several years later. He was imprisoned from 1964 to 11 February 1990. The day President F. W. De Klerk released Mandela from prison, Mandela had been incarcerated for 27 years for standing up for justice and truth.

In April 1994, Mandela was the presidential candidate of ANC, and in that first and all subsequent democratic general elections in South

Africa, he emerged the winner (Peace around the World, paw.ypteam.com/nelsonmadela-php). Subsequently, "On 10 May 1994, Nelson Mandela was inaugurated as South Africa's first democratically elected president" (Desmond Tutu, 1999, p. 9).

Peace Model

After his presidential inauguration, Mandela was faced with either taking revenge on the white minority that had, for many centuries, subjugated, dehumanized, and killed many of the black South Africans or to draw a program that could heal the battered black communities and usher in peace and progress in the entire nation of South Africa. The entire white communities, the blacks, the coloured people, and indeed the entire world waited for his decision. He startled the world when "he opted decisively for peace through reconciliation" (Kurien, Kunnumpuram, 2011, p. 233). Saddled with the onerous task of presiding over the transition from apartheid minority regime to a multicultural nascent democracy, Mandela was in no doubt that national reconciliation was to be the primary task of his government.

2.4. STEPHEN RICHARDS COVEY'S PEACE MODEL

(24 October 1932 – 16 July 2012)

Stephen R. Covey was an American educator, author, businessman, and a leadership speaker. Among his books, the most popular is *The Seven Habits of Highly Effective People*. Given the number of his works on leadership, he must be one of the world's greatest leadership experts. He was a professor at the Jon M. Huntsman School of Business at Utah State University until his death in 2012. Covey was born to Stephen Glenn Covey and Irene Louise Richards-Covey in Salt Lake City, Utah, on 24 October 1932.

What is known today as Covey's Peace Model is the project of his book entitled *The 3rd Alternative: Solving Life's Most Difficult Problems*. In his own view of the book, "It's about a principle so fundamental that I believe it can transform your life and the world."

Covey's Model of Peace

Covey opens his discourse with an assertion that there are always two sides or parties to a conflict. He claimed, "Most conflicts have two sides. We are used to thinking in terms of 'my team' against 'your team.' My team is good, your team is bad, or at least 'less good.' My team is right and just; your team is wrong and perhaps even unjust. My motives are pure; yours are mixed at best. In each case, there are two alternatives." He maintains there is a way out of "life's dilemmas and deep divisions," and "It's not your way, and it's not my way. It's a higher way. I call it 'the 3rd Alternative' " (Stephen, R. Covey, 2011, p. 8).

Since human beings are engrossed in this "2-Alternative thinking," the question is: "how can we ever get past it?" Covey is of the view that the root-cause of conflict lies in people's thinking system, that is, their thought paradigm which is often engrossed in egoistic tendency. Rising above this parochial, self-elating pattern of thinking enables us to see clearly 'an inclusive map' which incorporates the others' view. Hence, he proposes a map combination as the most effective means of actualizing peace.

CHAPTER THREE

EDEH'S CHARITY/ *MMADI* PEACE MODEL

The prevalence of wars, terrorism and nuclear armament that threaten the very foundation of world's existence places the search for peace on the lips of all and sundry. History carries upon itself the heavy burden of discord, dissension, hatred, violence, racial discrimination, wars, slavery, religious and cultural prejudices whose combined effects have consistently rendered most peace-ventures fruitless. In an era when man sees no reason and value in the continued existence of the other and would spend invaluable resources to procure instruments of life destruction, the gospel of peace becomes a priority for all concerned stakeholders. It is on the strength of this that Rev Fr Prof. E.M.P Edeh C.S.Sp. OFR from the cradle of his mission developed a Peace Model envisioned to possess the capacity of restoring the much sought world peace; a Peace Model that is unique. Edeh's Charity Peace Model is founded on the basis of his philosophy of *mmadi*. This chapter focuses its discussion on Edeh's Charity Peace Model.

3.1. EDEH'S *MMADI* PEACE MODEL

Every conflict has as its source the apparent diversity in people's perception and interpretation of reality. There is a correlation between conflict and people's thought systems in the sense that every conflict is a struggle to forcefully bend one party to accept the views and biddings of the others. Hence, by logic of extension, conflicts and strife build up from the mind. This psychological underpinning of conflicts calls for a revamping of people's thought systems for any Peace Model to prevail. This fact is accentuated in the UNESCO Constitution where it is averred that "since wars begin in the minds of men, it is in the minds of men that the defences of peace must be constructed" (UNESCO Constitution). This fact is further corroborated by Sachidanand, in his claim that "Culture of Peace and non-violence needs education systems and institutions that will help promote unity and peace within the individual, within family, within the nation and within the whole world" (A.J. Sachidauand, 2011, p. 98.). By education, it is meant a structure valid and strong enough to reset the thinking system of the makers of wars.

In consonant with the above stated fact, Edeh in his bid to establish an authentic peace model, developed a viable philosophy, part of which has come to be known as "Philosophy of Mmadi" (Agbo, et al., 2013, p. 35). The fundamental motive for the development of this philosophy is to tackle the problem of hatred and dissension from the root by bringing to the consciousness of people the sacrality of human ontology owing to its theocentric affinity and source. Edeh arrived at the central tenet of this philosophy through his metaphysical consideration of the being of man. He consequently reached the zenith of his investigation in the discovery of the Igbo concept of man: *mmadi*, from the Igbo word for man, *madu*. He holds that:

> "From the exposition of the word man (*madu*), we discover that in man the Igbo is able to discover the notion of "good that is" . . . the Igbo notion of "good that is" must be understood in the context of creation. To say that man is "good that is" is not to say that man is "good in se" for no one is "good in se" except God . . . Man is "good that is" in the sense that having been created by God, he is a product of his maker and hence shares in the being of his maker, the highest good" (Edeh, 1985, pp. 100-101).

The central point of Edeh's assertion is that, being a product of the supreme good, man has a spark of goodness in him; he is, ipso facto, ontologically good. A proper comprehension of this philosophy should quench every urge for conflict and strife in every rational human being. This is so because when one beholds goodness (as in man), there is an instant subconscious arousal to cherish, to love, to admire, to share in, and to care. In this state of mind, one can only think of peace, not war.

3.2. THE INDIVIDUAL TRANQUILLITY AS A BASIC CONSTITUENT OF EDEH'S CHARITY PEACE MODEL

Every society and the larger world are conglomerates of individuals of diverse psycho-social and biological make-ups. Thus, every reasonable peace talk and model must incontestably begin from sincere and practical consideration of the individual's inner tranquillity. Hence, world peace and the individual's inner peace are interlocked in a hermeneutical circular relationship in the sense that there cannot be a universal peace if the individual members are in a state of interior conflictual existence and the individual's inner peace is grossly threatened, if not eradicated, when the external world is trapped in unending wars and terrors. However, it makes more sense to state that the actualization of the inner tranquility of all the individual members of the world inevitably and effortlessly ushers in the much needed world peace. John Sachidanand accentuates this fact in his claim that "Peace within the individual is the basis of peace in the world" (Sachidauand, Op. cit., p.88).

In the perspective of Edeh's Peace Model, the individual's tranquillity is nothing short of a *conditio sine qua non* for a holistic and authentic peace model capable of tackling the problems challenging this global bride (world peace). Edeh has a peculiar view, both of the true nature and the most effective means of actualizing this individual tranquillity. Hence, he has erected numerous structures and initiatives with an enormous strength of instilling tranquillity and calming the intra-personal tension pervading the being of persons.

In his view, events, situations, persons, and things in the world gain access to one's consciousness via perceptual channels—both sensual and intuitive. The individual is confronted daily with realities of life within the lattice of socio-economic, political, and religious milieu. Sequel to that, any imbalance in the individual's relationship with these structures results in certain misfortunes and calamities such as: sickness, poverty, illiteracy, terrorism, etc., each of which is capable of eroding the individual's tranquillity. These existential malaises put the individual in an agitative and apprehensive mood, thereby poising him for war and other forms of unrest. In addition to the aforementioned,

Edeh ultimately attributes the cause of intra-personal tension and unrest to the individual's broken relationship with God, his maker and the ultimate source of interior peace. This, according to him, owes to the fact that "God is at the heart of every being as the being's Chi"— personal God (Edeh, 1985, p. 129). Consequently, any alteration in one's relationship with God emits an emptiness, an unwholesomeness that creates interior conflict, because according to St. Augustine, God has made us for himself and our souls can never rest until they rest in God. The foregoing lucidly portrays the fact that Edeh's Peace Model is cognizant of man's psycho-somatic components and suggests that for any model to restore man's inner peace, it must take care of his material and spiritual needs.

Inspired by this discovery and the ardent desire for an authentic peace model, Fr Edeh has established various structures intent on addressing both the spiritual and material worries of people in order to restore their inner tranquillity and peace. First of these initiatives is a gigantic Pilgrimage Centre for Eucharistic Adoration and Special Marian Devotion, located in Elele, Rivers State, Nigeria. It is a centre where millions of people from across the globe gather, both as individuals and groups, to mend their fences with God and get adequately ensconced from harsh spiritual and physical realities that corrode their inner peace. The Pilgrimage Centre has also spread its tentacles with its spiritual activities going on in countries like: America, Germany, London, the Philippines, etc. showing its global capacity and relevance.

The uniqueness of this peace model lies in the fact that it pursues a grass-root re-orientation of the individual person to live within the orbit of love and a reciprocated appreciation of the other as an ontologically dignified "good that is" (*mmadi*). However, the cog in the wheel of this mission is the fact that the individual is constantly battered by so many bewildering experiences such as armed robbery, terrorism, illiteracy, poverty, and other forms of man's inhumanity to man. Due to these harrowing experiences, the individual tends to accept that existence is all about war, conflict, hatred, intimidation and other ills that characterize the Hobbesian state of nature. It was in a bid to address this problem that Fr Edeh discovered his philosophy of *mmadi* (good that is) richly buried in the African world view. With the capacity of a genus, he has professionally developed this philosophy to an extent that it constitutes his Peace Model. The central tenet of this philosophy contends that the Igbo (African) word for man *mmadi* (good that is) is not just a mere linguistic expression but an endemic belief that man was created by an ultimate goodness and as such is ontologically good. Authentic human existence for Edeh entails bringing care and support wholeheartedly to man especially the sick, the suffering, the abjectly poor and the abandoned; it is a duty which everybody must uphold. Edeh has demonstrated the practical applicability of this philosophy by establishing institutions where love and charity are exhibited to a fault. These institutions and establishments include:

1. Centre for Peace, Justice, and Reconciliation
2. The Catholic Prayer Ministry (CPM)
3. Museum of Charms and Fetish Objects
4. National Pilgrimage Centre
5. Educational Institutions of all types
6. Medical Institutions
7. Skill Acquisition Centres, Projects and Industries
8. Achievement of Millennium Development Goals Through Edeh's Philosophy and Activities
9. Superservant Leadership
10. Development of Charity Peace and *Mmadi* Peace Models
11. Madonna International Charity Peace Award
12. Four Religious Congregations for continuity and perpetuation of the achievement of world peace.

The efficacy of charitable acts done in these establishments in fostering and re-orienting individuals to seek peace and comradeship has been confirmably tremendous. This is because, like Christ, Fr Edeh simply tells the beneficiaries to go and do the same. As the saying goes "the reward for love is love," the individuals who benefit from these acts of love especially the youths who, otherwise, would have been poised to unleash terror, are effectively disarmed and challenged to sue for peaceful co-existence.

3.3. EDEH'S INTRA-AND INTER-RELIGIOUS PEACE INITIATIVES

Religion is an activity that bears on human ontology and addresses transcendental issues beyond human capacity but relevant to human existence. Man is a being suspended in existential finitude and inundated with myriads of challenges which he, as a result of his limitations, cannot tackle. Man needs a being capable of healing him when all medical expertise is exhausted; he needs a being that can guarantee him happiness and joy in the midst of adversities; he needs a being that can answer his enigmatic questions of death and fate in the yonder world which undeniably perturb his soul, hence man's alignment to the divine via religion. The necessity of religion to man explains the hyper-sensitive issues relating to man and his religion. A considerable percentage of conflicts, wars, terrorism, hatred, and dissension including the Christian Crusades and Islamic Jihads recorded in world's history have religious under-pinnings. The hydra-headed nature of religious crisis and its connectedness to the "God of man's life" makes it a big issue and a mountain which every authentic peace model must overcome. A.J. Sachidanand shares in this view when he opines that "Peace in the world is impossible without peace among religions in the world. Global Peace will also remain a mirage without the active support and involvement of religions." Religious crisis ranges from internal squabbles about various doctrines and beliefs among different denominations and sects of individual religions to bigger conflicts among different major religions over territorial control, disposition towards non-adherents, and claim of superiority. The big question is: can there be a peace model resonant enough to resolve various intra-religious and inter-religious crises that militate against the actualization of real global peace?

A consideration of Edeh's Peace Model reveals that it is imbued with peace initiatives that can properly handle any form of intra-religious and inter-religious crisis. Edeh recognizes the sensitivity of religious disputes; hence, his peace model incorporates certain peace initiatives that transcend religious differences. First, Edeh in his philosophy projects that every human being whether black or white, rich or poor, strong or weak, Christian or Muslim, Catholic or Protestant, Buddhist or Hindu, etc. has a common creator who cares and desires the well-being of everybody, irrespective of one's religious mantra. This is deeply rooted in Edeh's explication of the African concept of God in which he argues that God is "Ose-buluwa," that is, "One who has a plan for each creature and an objective plan for the entire creation and who at the same time guides and directs the creatures to the realization of the purpose of their creation" (Edeh, 1985, p. 123). Edeh, therefore, argues that religions should first of all recognize this ontological dignity of man as deserving respect, care, and love in respect of man's affinity to God, his creator who is also the ultimate Being worshipped by most religions. He further submits that this peaceful co-existence of people within and outside different religions should be considered paramount in the growth and success of religious activities.

Fr Edeh has demonstrated equally in a practical way the possibility of this religious peace initiative aspect of his peace model in most of his institutions. For instance, in the Pilgrimage Centre, people from every possible religion on Earth are welcomed with equal and impartial attention. God has shown His approval of this—Edeh's intra- and inter-religious peace initiative—by granting favours, miracles, and wonders to people of different religious backgrounds who come in millions to the Pilgrimage Centre. Edeh also uses this forum to preach peace and tolerance to these people of other denominations (outside Catholic Church) and other religions outside Christianity. In addition, Fr Edeh has also instituted an initiative in all his universities and other schools which permits members of every denomination and religion to comfortably carry on their religious activities without fear. For instance, this initiative gave the Sultan of Sokoto, the political and religious head of Islamic religion in Nigeria, the impetus to send his child to Madonna University, Fr Edeh's school, which would have been impossible without the conviction of this religious peace initiative. The numerous graduates which Fr Edeh's schools have produced and will produce are effectively re-oriented by this peace initiative, to live in religious tolerance, and with this mentality, they disperse with this gospel of peace to all corners of the world. Here lies the uniqueness of Edeh's Peace Model in the religious aspect.

3.4. EDEH'S INTRA-AND INTER CULTURAL PEACE INITIATIVES

Cultural divide has been another source of conflict because it hinges on the being of a people as distinct from others. The most common definition of culture is "a people's way of life," a definition born out of culture's incorporation of a people's religion, art, belief system, education, music, technology, etc.

The complexity of cultural disputes springs from the fact that, most times, people's visions are blurred by their cultural inclination and are persuaded to think that their culture is the only proper way of living while every other way is a misnomer. This trend often graduates from abhorrence of specific cultural conducts of a people to total prejudice of the whole life of the people of such culture. The implication is often that whatever anybody from such culture does is intrinsically evil and not acceptable. This creates tension between individuals of a specific culture over little differences and among people of different cultures over complex divides.

Sequel to the above issue, Fr Edeh, in pursuance of a peace model holistic enough to actualize an authentic and boundless peace in the world, established in 1984 a Centre for Peace, Justice and Reconciliation where millions of complicated cultural rancours have been recorded to have been settled. The amazing difference in this peace initiative lies in its methodology of settling disputes leading to a "no victor no vanquished" outcome. In this Reconciliation Centre, Fr Edeh exhibits an unusual seraphic wisdom in resolving conflicts that have defiled the judicial intelligence and professionalism of judges of highly credible courts of law. This is evident in what has been consistently observed in the centre where, in some cases, the parties come with lawyers and judges who were unable to handle them. Fr Edeh does not only resolve these conflicts but goes further to explain and gives the judges new perspectives in handling such intractable cases. This has been most effective too.

Another intricate value of this peace initiative is that before Fr Edeh commences the hearing and settling of cases, he admonishes the parties to embrace dialogue and peace instead of fighting and hatred, after which he proceeds to hear and reconcile them. The results have never fallen short of joy, jubilation, and the embracing of each other by the parties, as the end is always "no victor, no vanquished" oriented. Individuals who abide by the peace injunctions of Fr Edeh always experience an unimaginable progress and inner peace in their careers, businesses, families, communities, and other endeavours, while those who violate these peace agreements always run back to the Centre to confess and ask for pardon as they often experience catastrophic chaos and retarded growth and development in all they do. This singular character of the Centre is the compelling force that drives people of diverse cultures to Fr Edeh's Centre for Peace and Reconciliation to have their cases settled there.

3.5. THE INTERNATIONAL EFFECTS OF FR EDEH'S PEACE INITIATIVES

As stated earlier, there is a correlative interaction between the individual's and the group's peace in the sense that the individual comes to the group with his internal state of mind which determines a lot about the peaceful nature of the group. By logic of extension, if nations enjoy internal peace but engage in wars with other nations, the internal peace remains at the brink of the grave because it is still their citizens that suffer the ravages of the international conflicts. Consequently every authentic peace model must have its tentacles stretchable to an international level. Edeh's Peace Model matches this standard by the capacity of its indices. Fr Edeh has international peace initiatives embedded in the Madonna International Charity Peace Award (MICPA), his brainchild. In his own words, Fr Edeh comments:

> This award, no matter how small, is to be given to whoever in the whole world has distinguished himself or herself in achieving peace in the modern world, peace in the hearts of many in the society through his or her works of practical and effective charity, that is, instigating, encouraging and practicing charity in its grassroots through unreserved and selfless cares and support of the most helpless members of

the society leading to peace in the hearts of many and thus peace to the modern world (Edeh, 2009, p.59).

The international character of the award is evidenced in the national diversities of the recipients which include:

1. Mrs. Chris Mary Maduka – Makurdi, Nigeria
2. Bishop Rene Maria Ehouzou – Benin Republic
3. Archbishop Kelvin Felix – Island of Haiti
4. Archbishop Fernando R. Capalla – Vietnam, Philippines
5. Leanghon Hoy (Buddhist) – Cambodia
6. Mr/Mrs Ray and Jill Wagner – Britain

Commenting on his vision about the Charity Peace Award, Fr Edeh remarked, "This is an award that has begun in a small way but hopefully, will grow to be world-renowned like the Nobel Peace Prize of Oslo in Norway."

3.6. PRACTICAL APPLICATION OF EDEH'S CHARITY/ *MMADI* PEACE MODEL

To do justice to this chapter, it is important that one goes back to the very origin of the Centre for Peace, Justice, and Reconciliation, Elele, where Fr Edeh presides over complex cases on a regular basis. Elele that now rings a bell in the world used to be one of the most remote and obscure villages in Rivers State, Nigeria, and was associated with being one of the dumping grounds for most of the victims of the Nigerian-Biafran War. Consequently, most of the inhabitants abandoned their homes and fled as the land was littered with dead bodies and unattended sick people.

There was no food in the land and many were dying of hunger and kwashiorkor. People were homeless, many maimed, rejected, and dejected. There was no functional school, hospital, or even market. Consequently, death in intervals of hours had taken its toll on mankind (cf. History of the Pilgrimage Centre, p.13).

A beam of light started shining into the shadowy land with the arrival of Fr Prof. Edeh in Elele in 1984 as the parish priest of Our Lady of Lourdes' parish. Confronted with the inhuman condition of these people, it became obvious to this dynamic pastor that "good homilies" alone could not help the people's plight. Accordingly, he delved into effective care of the sick, feeding of the hungry, and offering of shelter for the homeless. At this, everyone within the vicinity breathed a sigh of relief that at last, liberation had come. Little did they know that this was just but a preamble of the marvellous things to come in future (Edeh, 2012, p.13).

When the people realized Edeh's willingness to empathize with them in their situations, they spared him no rest. They began flocking to him first in tens, then in hundreds, then in thousands seeking help for their different needs. Many families, villages and towns set against each other by the Nigeria-Biafran War brought cases of land dispute and others property for settlement. Fr Edeh would seat hours of unending mediating and amicably settle their cases. Orphans and destitutes who had no homes came to him for shelter and care. Fr Edeh readily made shift-houses, like tents, for them and cared for them spiritually and materially. For the sick and the injured, he would provide medic-care, wash and bandage their wounds. The place became haven for all suffering people; once they came, many would not go back as they had practically no place to go. Holy masses, prayers, consultations, confessions, and dispensing of other sacraments and sacramentals formed part of the spiritual care. All over the country, the name Fr Edeh became a household name, described as a priest who became all things to all men (cf. National Pilgrimage Centre, Elele, The Journey So Far, p. 6).

When the then Bishop of Port Harcourt Diocese, Rt Rev Dr Fitzgibbon of Blessed Memory came visiting, after staying with Fr Edeh and watching what he was doing—how many people he was living and working with, those he fed himself, the many blessings and favours of God on the people—he marvelled and said "All I have seen is Catholic, all the activities are centered on prayer; in fact, it is a ministry inspired by the Holy Spirit, therefore the place should be called 'Catholic Prayer Ministry of the Holy Spirit.' " As the number of people kept increasing, it became impossible for the parish premises to accommodate them and also for Fr Edeh to combine attending to their needs and running the parish. This made the then Bishop of Port-Harcourt Diocese, and the then Superior of the Holy Ghost Fathers to separate the activities of the ministry from the parish. The bishop also advised Fr Edeh to look for a land separate from the parish in order to accommodate the teeming population. He accepted the advice and acquired a piece of land. The Catholic Prayer Ministry left the parish lands of Our Lady of Lourdes and moved into the new acquired land in 1989 when the Bishop of Port Harcourt blessed and inaugurated the new site. The foundation stone of the Centre was consequently blessed by Pope John Paul II on 22 March 1998 at Oba in Onitsha during the beatification of Blessed Michael Iwene Tansi.

3.7.   THE CENTRE FOR PEACE, JUSTICE AND RECONCILIATION, ELELE

As aforementioned, Fr Edeh, on his return from America and further studies, saw people in devastating conditions such as hunger, sickness, conflicts, death, etc. He took it upon himself to listen to these people as they narrated their different cases involving land disputes, disagreement among business partners, family crises and so on. The settlement of these cases gave birth to what is now referred to as the Centre for Peace, Justice, and Reconciliation in Elele, where over fourteen million cases have been peacefully settled with no charges.

It is worth mentioning here that this Centre, which began in 1984, is the first of its kind in the world. Again, through this Centre, myriads of families in discord and business partners have been reconciled. This humble man of God is directly involved in this effort; he visits families, villages, and towns that are having conflicts (if invited) and listens to them with love and compassion and offers advice, guidelines, and prayers. In the Centre, he regularly takes his seat to mediate between conflicting parties (Amah, 2013).

The Centre for Peace, Justice, and Reconciliation later became a sub-centre in the National Pilgrimage Centre. Describing this Centre and the main function of the reconciliation unit (Edeh, 2007, p. 10), the Founder and Director of the Centre says as quoted by Udaya, (2013):

"This (Reconciliation Unit) is an important office to which various people, families, kindreds, people from various offices, Catholics, non-Catholics, Christians, Muslims, and followers of African Traditional Religion are steadily coming to reconcile among themselves, achieving the peace that law courts and traditional courts cannot gain for the society, namely lasting peace among peoples, individuals, families, clans, kindreds, and towns."

In this unit which is strategically located within the Pilgrimage Centre, Elele, a remarkable result was recently recorded over the assassination case of one Mr. Oliver Nwagbara by an unknown person. When Mr. Oliver was assassinated, many people were suspected. Close friends and family members were pointing accusing fingers at one another. All other means of settling disputes were used to no avail. As a last resort, the family members and friends of the late Mr. Oliver agreed to come to Elele for the resolution of the dispute and reconciliation.

In the article *Practical Application of Edeh's Charity Peace Model*, Udaya presented the case. Peter O. Amah, a lecturer at Gonzaga University in Washington, USA, coincidentally visited Edeh's Peace Centre during his research on servant leaders in Africa and witnessed the process. While writing, now not merely as an armchair researcher but most importantly as a living witness to the reconciliation and peace brought by Edeh in May 2011, he discusses how a murder case that had lasted for many years in the law courts without success was settled and resolved in Elele. It all happened in his presence in the reconciliation unit within the Pilgrimage Centre of Eucharistic Adoration and Special Marian Devotion, in Elele, Nigeria.

When the family members and friends of the slain Mr Oliver arrived at the reconciliation unit Elele, Edeh listened to them attentively and empathically and in a non-judgmental approach. It is a firm conviction in Elele that every case can be settled and peace is possible in every situation. The main thing is that people have to be reminded of certain facts which include: the ontological goodness of all human beings as *mmadi*, the possibility of people making mistakes even though they are fundamentally good creatures, the need for forgiveness, and the willingness of the Centre to help all people recover from whatever might have happened to them.

In response to their sides of the story, as noted by (Amah, 2012, pp. 23-24), Edeh, the founder and director said:

"All of you have come here today and are here to make peace, and we will commend all these things into God's hand. Homicide is a big thing and when it occurs, there is often confusion regarding who committed the crime. You have all laid your complaints and God will take absolute control of the situation.

"In all circumstances and at all stages, the ordinary as well as the extraordinary ministers of the peace process in Elele recognize the role of the unseen power of the Prince of Peace in reconciling quarrelling parties. Most people know it very well and believe it firmly that it is not solely human beings who do the work of peace in Elele. Both the founding father of the peace process and all his collaborators are but instruments in the hands of God."

Udaya maintains in his article that nobody advertises the Reconciliation Centre, Elele, in any radio or television stations or even in newspapers. Yet the fame spreads like wildfire to all parts of the country and beyond. People carry the message as they go back to their homes testifying how effective Edeh's method works in all circumstances and this spreads to all and sundry. It is very clear that once any group or groups of people come down to Elele, there is always hope that their case or cases would be solved.

Amah (2012, p. 25) confirms that "the murder case stated above had been in the law court for more than a decade without any resolution. Those involved spent their savings with no guarantee of satisfaction." Yet the same case was settled in the Peace Centre in Elele without any financial cost to the parties involved. At the end of the settlement, all became very happy, shook hands and embraced one another as their sign of total settlement of the case, reconciliation with one another, forgiveness of each other, and total reconstruction and recognition and acceptance of each other's worth as *mmadi* deserving care of each other as God (Chineke) cares for all.

3.8.   CHARACTERISTICS OF EDEH'S PEACE MODEL

Returning of Relationship to Original State

Among other things, Edeh's Peace Model differs from all other methods or models by virtue of what it achieves at the end of the day—the returning of relationship to the original state. People are usually reconciled and returned into the original state of their relationship in which they were before their quarrel or dispute. This is shown by the enthusiastic embrace and the kiss of peace given to one another and their pledges to remain in the new found peace immediately after reconciliation in the unit.

This model stands at variance with the court rulings where, after litigations and counter-litigations, the quarrelling parties would resort to other dangerous and diabolical means, especially those who were not favoured in the court. What obtains in Elele, thanks to Edeh's method, is distinctive because the people are forever refreshed and renewed in their relationship at the end of the peace deal.

The Situation of 'No Victor No Vanquished'

Normally when a case is taken to the court of law, at the end of the day there must be a winner and a loser. This is different from what obtains in Edeh's golden model. It does not follow the court method whereby one of the parties wins whereas the other loses in the case. The model does not primarily seek out the blameless and the blameworthy ones in the quarrel; rather, in dealing with the issue at stake, it aims at bringing one to the consciousness of ontological goodness of all humans, equality of all, the natural imperative of all to love all and the futility of human conflicts.

Edeh usually points out whatever mistakes each person might have made in the light of the "good in se" and "the good per se." Surely, the process is not entirely judgmental since the foundation is based on forgiveness and charity. This is made clear to all the parties through counselling. This model does not sentence or acquit anyone, for it is anchored on forgiveness. When a wrongdoer comes back from doing what is bad, it is normal under the demands of *mmadi* that the old things he or she did be forgiven and forgotten entirely. Through this means everlasting peace is procured or recovered (Udaya, 2013).

Recovery of Everlasting Peace

The normal thing is that all the people concerned agree among themselves to come down to Elele for reconciliation. Peace Centre in Elele never forces anybody to come, but God can act through His own mysterious ways. Under normal circumstances, all those involved in any case, be it a land case, marriage case, business case, etc., come to Elele in order to consult with Edeh or any of his collaborators at the Centre with the firm conviction that they are going to the last resort. It is on record that the new covenant of peace which every disputing party to the quarrel enters into in the name and presence of the "good in se" lasts forever. By the people's own free will and faith, the peaceful co-existence previously lacking due to the dispute would be recovered and returned.

Udaya insists that the conclusion of Amah (2012) is correct and accurate: "Edeh provides service free of charge so that advantages of status or monetary influence are eradicated to give way to mutual dialogue, fair play, understanding, forgiveness, peace, and reconciliation." What needs to be added here is that since the reconciliation process is not solely a human arrangement and the "good in se" gives all His gifts free of charge, then it is proper that the peace process be delivered to all people free of charge. And that is exactly what Edeh does at Elele and likewise teaches his collaborators to do. It is really the "good in se" who brings quarrelling people here, the same "good in se" reconciles using His humble ministers and as such it naturally demands no payment. This rule is strictly kept.

3.9. PRACTICAL RESULTS OF EDEH'S CHARITY PEACE MODEL

In his book *The First Articulation of African Philosophy*, Edeh insisted that Africans act in their thinking and think in their action and went on to maintain that any thought bereft of action is not qualified to be termed *African* (Edeh, 2009). Since Edeh's Model of Peace derives from African philosophy whereby theory and practice are inseparable, it is expected that it must have borne fruits over the years. This Model of Peace has been applied in so many areas of life ever since it was established in the mid-eighties. The Centre for Peace, Justice, and Reconciliation has treated successfully so many cases from diverse classes and creeds. In what follows, we shall discuss some of these areas where remarkable successes have been recorded. We shall present a few of the cases as carefully examined by Udaya (2013).

a. In the Area of Business

One business man named Chief Francis Arinze from Oraukwu, Idemili, in Anambra State, had a problem with his help-mates. One day the help-mates were told to carry a lorry load of paint which the man produces from Onitsha to Aba in Abia State for supply. On reaching Mgbidi, a town in Imo state lying between Anambra and Abia states, they stopped over to eat. In less than three minutes, when they came out from the eatery, they could not find the lorry or the paint. Upon the disappearance, they returned to Onitsha to report to their Chief Arinze. The following morning, they reported the matter to the Anambra State police force who then combed the city of Orlu and its Environs. Subsequently, they recovered the lorry, though without the buckets of paint. The lorry also had lost three of its tyres.

Consequently, the suspects—Chief Arinze's help-mates—were taken to the State Criminal Investigation Department of the Nigeria Police Department at Awka for further interrogation and investigation. For over a long period of time, running into months, nothing was really discovered and no appreciable progress made in terms of reconciling the people involved. When all civil or secular means to solve the problem failed to work, the director of the company resolved to come to Elele. He came and was given appointment papers to invite all those connected with the missing buckets of paint. They came and were allowed to air their views. They were asked some pertinent questions regarding the lorryload of paint. All of them denied having any knowledge of the missing paint. Then they swore an oath before God as Edeh's model demanded. Even those members of the company who were not at the scene of the crime and were the least suspected such as the Accountant General swore in the name of God that none of them had any connection with the missing paint. Something mysterious happened that taught everybody a big lesson. The founding chairman of the paint company was defending the Accountant General and almost refused him taking part in the oath-taking. But barely one week after the swearing before God, the least-suspected Accountant General came back to the Reconciliation Office crying like a little child. When he was asked why, he confessed to be one of those responsible for stealing from Chief Francis.

According to him, he had taken huge sum of money from the director's treasury through all means available. He confessed to all the forgeries he had previously done—the master's bank stamp, the man's signature and those of the bank manager and cashier. Furthermore, he said that what worried him most was that there had never been anything he requested from Chief Francis that he refused to do for him. Finally, both the key suspects, the driver, the conductor, and others, plus the least-suspected ones, were summoned back a second time. The confession was communicated to them and after due counselling and corrections, they were reconciled amicably free of charge. All of them returned home happily.

In an oral interview with Mr John Uguru on 28 May 2012 (John is a married man of over fifty years of age from Ebonyi state, Nigeria, who has been working in the Reconciliation Unit of the Pilgrimage Centre in Elele since 1986), he had this to say:

> "What gives me joy in this reconciliation espoused by Edeh is that it instils peace and joy in the hearts of those involved and most of the time they go back home happily. In addition, those who benefit from the peace and reconciliation process

in Elele normally recommend it to others who would not hesitate in coming to Elele with their own cases."

Further, commending the model established by Edeh, which he has been part of for the past twenty years, Mr. John (2012) thundered:

"Even pagans and adherents of other religions sometimes get converted from their denominations to the Catholic Church after such an encounter. In a similar vein, lukewarm Christians who attend the reconciliation events normally get themselves rejuvenated and revived as far as their faith in God is concerned."

b. A Land Case between the Mgbalukwu-isu and Ogboji-Ezzagu Communities in Ebonyi State

Two communities in the Onicha and Ishielu local government areas of Ebonyi State were fighting with dangerous weapons over a piece of land belonging to them for over ninety-seven (97) years. This quarrel left many people dead and many more deformed. Due to the fertility of the land, no party was ready to give up. As a matter of fact, heads rolled due to fighting with guns and cutlasses.

Various regimes of state government right from the times of the old Eastern Regional Government, Anambra State Government, Enugu State Government, and finally Ebonyi State Government did not succeed in solving the problem or reconciling the people. Policemen and other agents sent to maintain law and order did not make any headway either.

The war over the land continued until a new parish priest arrived in the area in the person of Rev Fr Michael Agwu, the then new parish priest of St Michael's Catholic Church Isu-Onicha. On arrival, Fr Agwu saw the ugly situation, heard the history of failed attempts and decided to come to Elele for assistance. He came; he saw Edeh and explained the whole matter to him. Edeh obliged by going to the troubled area with his peace message and model.

On arrival, he gathered the people, counselled all of them in the light of *mmadi,* and told them the need to make peace. After his usual teaching on the need for peace and other practices, the people accepted to end the case that day. They all swore before God that none of them will ever kill or destroy any *mmadi.*

Something else happened later that made everybody marvel at the efficacy of the peace deal. The sponsor of the wanton disregard for *mmadi* (human life) and a native of one of the communities who was supplying arms from overseas died mysteriously while agitating against the peace deal. Also, a group of boys who rose against the peace agreement did not live to carry out their plans against *mmadi.*

As a result of these awesome and mysterious events after the visit of Edeh, fear gripped everybody and all of them came together again and agreed never to spill the blood of *mmadi* over the piece of land. Finally, peace returned to both communities. Today, it is not just that peace has been achieved; both communities now inter-marry which is the highest expression of solidarity and reconciliation. No more war, or fighting, or quarrelling regarding that land again.

Furthermore, commenting on the effectiveness of Edeh-Elele peace process, Sir Patrick Ndubaku Snr (2012) said, "I feel happy when I see people accept the peace deal which is never forced on them. The peace process is useful to all and sundry as it brings about progress in all aspects of the society." By implication no one forces any one into the system of peace and such process creates an atmosphere for development of the whole *mmadi*. Additionally, the chairman of the Centre for Reconciliation, Ndubaku (2012) assuredly said:

> "It is objective. No one influences the other or is influenced by the other person or minister. Every case is treated objectively by a neutral minister who operates in the framework of *mmadi* which does not admit favouritism. This objective character appeals to everybody and makes all people interested in the Elele peace process. This explains why highly placed people in the society send quarrelling parties to Elele. The objective nature also draws people

from all religious backgrounds since no one is discriminated against in treating any case."

c. A Land Dispute between Ugbene and Ugbenu in Anambra State

Ugbene and Ugbenu are two nearby communities in Anambra State. The communities are descendants of two brothers from the same parents. They had a land dispute which resulted in their separation and change of names. The land dispute lasted for fifty-eight (58) years during which many people from both communities were mercilessly killed.

One day, in the early 90s, some sensible boys (youths) from both communities decided to seek peace so as to avoid the killings going on over the particular piece of land. Those boys were influenced by Edeh's peace speeches during the Pilgrimage Week activities in Elele, which they attended. When they came to Elele, they made their intention for peace and reconciliation known to the Reconciliation Unit. To that effect, they were given an invitation letter to bring the elders from both communities down to the Reconciliation Centre.

When the appointed time came, the elders from both communities journeyed to Elele. The elders were ten in number from each community. When they arrived, they were interrogated and the issue was traced back to the origin, and the people reconciling the case found out that both communities were originally from the same parents.

In that light, they were instructed to stop killing one another since they are of the same blood, and they were instructed under the *mmadi* world view to share the land into two and each of them will take one. Initially, they were not keen in accepting the decision to end the case, but later on they did—for they agreed to share the land between the two communities and that was how the dispute came to an end. All the killings stopped as they took an oath and entered into covenant that they would not fight again over the land.

Chapter Four

EDUCATIONAL/ ECONOMIC EMPOWERMENT OF THE YOUTH AND SOCIETAL STABILITY

Father Emmanuel Edeh has been exceptional in establishing a wide range of youth empowerment programmes that add more value to the quality of life and well-being of these youths and more than meet the aims and objectives of the Millennium Development Goals. Many of these programmes predate the promulgation of the Millennium Development Goals. In other words, Fr Edeh not only had the vision of these needs but had started doing something about them many years before the current advocates of the Millennium Development Goals woke up the idea (cf. *The Challenges of Sustainability of Fr Emmanuel Edeh's Youth Empowerment Programmes: The Pros and Cons of Charismatic Leadership,* An unpublished article by Remy N. Onyewuenyi, CSSp, Ph. D., 2013, P. 1).

These programmes, according to Onyewuenyi, are life-enhancing and spirit-lifting. To say the least, they are good. Whatever is good must not only go round but must endure, be sustained. This author has written extensively on Fr Edeh's youth empowerment and poverty alleviation programmes and their related impacts in previous works such as: *Emmanuel M P Edeh: Man of Peace, His Life and Works* (2010); *Servant-Leader Emmanuel M P Edeh: An Inspiration in Youth Empowerment & Poverty Alleviation, The Nigerian Experience* (2011); and *The Spatio-Socio-Economic Impacts of Emmanuel Edeh's Philosophy of Practical and Effective Charity* (2011).

Concept of Empowerment and Poverty Alleviation

Remy Onyewuenyi (2013) quoted Rappaport in his book *In Praise of Paradox: A Social Policy of Empowerment Over Prevention* describes empowerment as a "construct that links individual strengths and competencies, natural helping systems, and proactive behaviours to social policy and social change." Empowerment connotes participation with others to achieve goals, efforts to gain access to resources that are very critical to growth and development. It entails giving power and authority to individuals which pave way for them to exercise their abilities and make powerful and valid contributions to a process.

Wikipedia, The Free Encyclopedia (2011) explains youth empowerment as "an attitudinal, structural and cultural process whereby young people gain the ability, authority and agency to make decisions and implement change in their own lives and the lives of other people." Youth empowerment connotes a gateway to intergenerational equity, civic engagement, and democracy building. It entails individual participation and contribution of youths in the growth and development effort.

Remy further maintains that youth empowerment aims at addressing the oppression, stratification, and inequality found among youth. It also focuses at providing youths with the opportunities and means to genuinely serve others in society and grow into confident leaders. Empowering the youth is not simply a matter of providing the right incentives for personal investment and guaranteeing returns, it is a bit more of providing the individual youth with the means to effectively adapt to change.

Commonwealth of Nations in Commonwealth Plan of Action for Youth Empowerment (2007-2015) sees youth empowerment as a state when young people "acknowledge that they have or can create chances in life, are aware of the implications of these choices, make informal decisions, and accept responsibility for the consequences of those actions. Empowering young people means creating and supporting the enabling conditions under which young people can act on their own behalf and their own terms, rather than at the direction of others."

Educational Empowerment

Fr Edeh has no rival in his conceptualization of and implementation strategies for youth empowerment through educational programmes. His contributions here are immense and multi-facetted. In the main, through his educational programmes he has contributed and is still contributing in no small measure to youth empowerment by providing structures and programmes that are capable of offering youths sound and holistic education, the type of education that truly equips the youth with the requisite skills and exposure to face the future and workplace with greater confidence and competence.

However, to do proper justice on how Edeh empowered the youth educationally, it is of paramount importance to do an exposition of some facts about education in Nigeria.

4.1. SOME FUNDAMENTAL FACTS ABOUT EDUCATION IN NIGERIA

Long before the Europeans arrived, formal education had not been part of Nigeria. The children were taught about their culture, social activities, survival skills, and work. Most of these education processes were imparted to the children informally; few of these societies gave a more formal teaching of the society and culture.

European education was introduced into Nigeria in the 1840s. It began in Lagos, Calabar, and other coastal cities. In a few decades, schooling in the English language gradually took roots in Nigeria. During the Colonial years, Great Britain did not promote education. The schools were set up and run by Christian Missionaries.

In the northern part of Nigeria, which was predominantly Muslim, Western education was prohibited. The religious leaders did not want the missionaries' interfering with Islam. This gave way to establishing Islamic schools that focused primarily on the Islamic education.

Prior to Nigeria's independence, Nigeria had only two established post-secondary institutions. Yaba Higher College (founded in 1934, later on Yaba College of Technology); and the University of Ibadan, founded in 1948. It was then a college of the University of London until two years after independence when she became autonomous. More prominent universities which include: University of Nigeria, Nsukka, Obafemi Awolowo University (formerly University of Ife), Ahmadu Bello University, and University of Lagos were founded in the years that followed the independence. In the 1970s, more universities were founded which included: University of Benin (founded in 1970), Calabar, Ilorin, Jos, Port Harcourt, Sokoto, and Maiduguri. In the 1980s, more universities were opened as well as institutes specializing in agriculture and technology. A number of polytechnics were also opened, which include the Yaba College of Technology, Lagos, and Kaduna Polytechnic, Kaduna.

The present decline in the Nigerian education system can be traced back to the 1980s and 1990s having its root in poor management of both human and economic resources. This grossly affected the schools.

4.2. THE GOVERNMENT TAKEOVER OF MISSIONARY SCHOOLS AND ITS EFFECTS

From the above background, the formal education in Nigeria came from the already-developed educational system through the Catholic and Protestant missionaries who owned the greater percentage of schools. The missionaries had focused objectives, sense of direction, and clear ideas about what kind of education, morals, and discipline to impart on their pupils and students. From early 70s to late 80s, the government, ill-advised by incompetent persons, gradually ejected the white missionaries and forcefully took over the schools.

The after-effects of the Nigerian civil war (6 July 1967 – 15 January 1970), include the collapse of the education system. This situation was the result of "taking over of schools" from the Missionaries and other bodies that were managing the schools. All primary and secondary schools, training colleges, and the likes all belonging to the churches and individuals in the country were appropriated without any form of compensation from the government.

4.3. THE OUTCOME OF THE SCHOOL "TAKE–OVER" BY THE NIGERIAN GOVERNMENT

The importance of education to human beings cannot be over-emphasized. Education is a human right that should be enjoyed by all human beings solely by reason of being human. There are lots of international human rights agencies that provide for education as a fundamental human right. Africa is one of the developing continents in the world. It is a truism that before a country is said to be developed, her educational managerial standard must be remarkably on a positive note; meaning that education must be the priority of the government. Unfortunately, the "take-over" of schools brought Nigerian education to an unimaginable degradation. Far from the above thought about education industry, Edeh clearly states that anybody who goes into the education industry for profit is missing the mark because the basic point in education, according to him, is to "train or mould the human person without counting the cost" (*Madonna International Journal of Research* Vol. 3 no. 1, SSN 1592-9830, May 2010).

Evidently, ever since the "take-over" of schools by the Nigerian government, the educational system has suffered a major setback and the governments systematically drained education of its substance beginning from the primary to the tertiary institutions. The practical result of the situation is the endemic corruption and a general state of lawlessness that characterize the educational system.

The deterioration of the school system continued unabated such that the system produced what one may call half-baked graduates. The so-called graduates—the products of the corrupt system—carry with them, into the entire system, the evil of corruption and the culture of low productivity. There was a rapid drop in the standard of education as a result of general lack of discipline on the part of students and the teachers or lecturers with little or no commitment to their employment. At that period, too, there were incessant strikes that became the order of the day. The effect was that students had to spend some wasteful number of years in schools before graduating and sometimes not even sure of graduating in any course of study.

Following from the above, even the government-owned tertiary institutions were mismanaged; funds were being siphoned into the pockets of few individuals. The condition was unbearable. The school system was so bad and life in the tertiary institutions was no longer guaranteed. Security of lives and property was nobody's business. The reasons were not farfetched. Since there was no discipline, government-owned tertiary institutes became safe asylums for all kinds of criminal activities. Schools were soon known for cultism and with all forms of cultic (criminal) activities—maiming, killing, raping, spiritualism, assassination, armed robbery, prostitution, and the like. They hijacked the education system, and under the disguise of "students' freedom of association," formed different rival cultic groups. Accordingly, "what began as a "free association of students" soon degenerated into a "pack of wolves," a "brood of armed robbers," an "army of bandits," and a "gang of terrorists and hired assassins" (Edeh, 2010, p. 1).

The question is: what is the way out of these horrendous situations? The next chapter provides answers to this question. It shall discuss Edeh's philosophy of education and many giant strides he has achieved in the education sector that have, to great extent, practically revamped education system in Nigeria.

4.4.   THE QUEST TO ESTABLISH THE FIRST POLYTECHNIC AND COLLEGE OF EDUCATION IN NIGERIA

Society is used to the practice of referring value re-orientation to social institutions such as the family (home), the school, religion, and government. This practice has been in order and had worked admirably well in Nigeria just before the civil war. The general sense of educational disorder and insecurity of lives and property resulting from the total collapse of morality at the end of the war was a call for serious concern. It was not just a re-examination of the whole issue, but a new solution to the unfortunate situations. In his attestation, Nwosu traced that "since 1982 when Ethical Revolution made its debut, we (Nigerians) have had the War Against Indiscipline (WAI), the Mass Agency for Mobilization, Social and Ethical Revolution (MAMSER) and the National Orientation Agency (NOA)" (*Journal of School of Education; Federal College of Education,* Eha-Amufu, vol.1, no. 2). The inability of all these agencies to deal with corruption and decadence in education sector (especially the tertiary institutions) is one among other reasons why there was a serious need for the intervention of the private bodies.

The first ever non government-owned tertiary institution in Nigeria, Our Saviour Institute of Science, Agriculture, and Technology (OSISATECH) Polytechnic and College of Education, was born out of the zeal and concern to the suffering youths and the physically challenged persons. It was also a quick and appropriate response to the late Pope John Paul II's appeal for Catholic universities in his "*Ex Corde Ecclesiae*" (educational advancement of the people of God) in 1990. Edeh reacts thus; "Given the precarious situation of the educational system in the country, the need to arrest the fast-growing decay in education in Nigerian Universities became an issue not only for the government, but also for other stakeholders; not only for the parents but also for the generality of the public... hence the yearning and invitation to individuals and groups to lend a helping hand to government in re-building educational system" (2009, p. 174).

As a leading figure in education in Nigeria, Fr Edeh took a painstaking frontier in the annals of the Nigerian educational system. It was a noticeable struggle with the "powers that be" who never believed that an individual could delve into starting a tertiary institution in this part of the world. However, with Edeh's determination, in October 1989, OSISATECH Polytechnic was established by "Edict No. 18 of 1989," (Edeh,1998, p. 154). On 6 November 1989, the first students of the institution started lectures.

The testimony of Prof. Romanus Unegbu, the first Rector of the Institution after Fr Edeh gives the picture of the zealous and resilient effort of the founder (Edeh) to proffer some remedy to the condition of the educational system at the moment. He has this to say: "My first encounter with our Saviour through the educational sector of the Catholic Prayer Ministry is still a mystery to me. It was on November 4, 1990, at precisely 11:30 pm when I had already gone to bed, that I had a knock at my door…, when I asked what was wrong, I was told that Rev Fr Edeh wished to see me. Not knowing Fr Edeh too well at that time, I asked them whether they knew who they were looking for. Their answer was "Are you not Professor Unegbu?" "When does he want to see me and where?" I asked. They replied, "Now, at No. 1 Ogui Road." When I was finally ushered into his office where he worked tirelessly night and day, he said: "Yes, Professor, I sent for you. Students will be arriving here on November 6th and I want you to draw up the timetable for them to start lectures immediately when they arrive." At this point, several questions came to mind to ask, but I was unable to ask any! The only one I managed to ask was "When do I start?" He replied, "Now." Thus, he continued, "I took my work as the Vice Rector of this great Institution whilst Fr Edeh was the Rector. He handed over the office as Rector to me in 1996 after he had handled the institution personally for six years" (Ngwoke, I. K. B., *Jesus the Saviour in Our Midst*, pp. 153-154). Today, OSISATECH Polytechnic as a preverbal mustard seed has grown to full maturity with all the programmes fully accredited to the glory of God and now has two campuses both in Enugu State, Nigeria.

4.5. THE QUEST TO ESTABLISH THE FIRST PRIVATE UNIVERSITY IN WEST AFRICA

The establishment of the OSISATECH Polytechnic and College of Education came as an "eye opener" and a welcome relief to parents. In 1993, when it was thought that state law could charter a private university, Fr Edeh struggled and got the approval of Anambra State government to begin Madonna University. As a consequence, Madonna University became the first and only private university in the country at that time.

Within the same period, Fr Edeh concluded negotiation with the then Enugu State Government for the establishment of Saviour University at Enugu. But before the official pronouncement of Saviour University in

Enugu, a federal law which prevented the state authority from chartering private universities came into force in 1994.

This conservative federal law not only aborted the prospects of Saviour University at Enugu, but also made the situation very difficult for the already existing Madonna University. Fr Edeh had to go back to the drawing board and start all over what had been virtually completed.

Edeh Narrates His Experience as Follows:

In drafting the federal law for the establishment of private universities, the law makers came up with very stringent measures and rules that apparently aimed at stifling all private efforts to establish universities in the country. Requirements that were necessary and those that were not actually necessary were all imposed. I was the unfortunate one used as the guinea pig. But I was not discouraged. With unflinching confidence and faith in Jesus the Saviour and Mary, Mother of Jesus the Saviour, I, dogged in my resolve, set out and struggled indefatigably to meet all the requirements.

By 1994, after all difficulties, Edeh was able to convince the then military Head of State General Ibrahim Babangida, to permit the then Attorney General of the Federation, Honorable Justice Clement Akpangbo, to draw up the federal law enabling, for the first time, the establishment of private universities in the country. Hence, Edict (Law) No. 29 that permits the establishment of the private universities in Nigeria was drawn and approved.

In the same year, 47 applications were sent in by various groups and individuals proposing to be authorized to establish private universities in Nigeria. Various stringent rules and regulations were being issued progressively one after the other. Consequently, by 1995, all the proposing stakeholders apparently gave up. The office of the National Universities Commission, Abuja, wrote in one of its 1995 publications that only Madonna University had persevered in providing all the requirements. After seven tedious years of intensive struggle, the federal government of Nigeria finally approved Madonna University on 20 April 1999. The certificate of establishment and approval to operate as a fully fledged university was received from the federal government in a colourful ceremony organized by the Federal Ministry of Education at Abuja. Madonna University was born, alive and healthy, bouncing and bubbling. On 22 May 1999, Madonna University took off to a healthy start, thus becoming the first private university to be established in Nigeria and the first Catholic university in the West African region. The emergence of the university in the country during a time that the public university system was undergoing unprecedented decay, was a welcome relief to all teeming youths and parents yearning for a proper and well-seasoned university education.

The university began with four foundation faculties and a college. These are the Colleges of Medicine and Health Sciences, Faculty of Law, Faculty of Engineering and Technology, Faculty of Management and Social Sciences, and Faculty of Education. Madonna University soon became one of the fastest growing universities in the world. It is the first private university in Nigeria that has deemed it fit to tackle the academic and moral problems of thousands of school leavers, who otherwise would have roamed the streets in utter frustration, constituting nuisance and adding to the already existing over-population of criminals and hoodlums in the society. Today Madonna University is a household name and the most vibrant private and Catholic university in Nigeria and the West African region. Interestingly, Madonna University has three great campuses situated in Anambra, Enugu, and Rivers States respectively.

4.6. EDEH'S ROLE IN NIGERIA'S EDUCATIONAL SECTOR

The presence of Edeh in the Nigerian educational system did wake both the government and private stakeholders from slumber. With the relentless struggle exhibited, Edeh has taken the noble role of leading this part of the world—Nigeria specifically—out of the shamble condition of the educational system.

Edeh came on board when all hope for the education of the youth was almost dead. He salvaged education in Nigeria and set her free from the era of monopoly by the government and from the degenerating condition of the few students who were lucky to be in school. Before Edeh's involvement in the Nigerian educational sector and after the takeover of schools by government, it was obvious that the few tertiary institutions were being turned into a breeding ground for crimes of all sorts. They were "places where students kill and are being killed" (Melladu, 2011, p. 94) on a daily basis, cultism, sorting for marks, malpractice, and other forms of corruption that were almost part and parcel of the daily activities in the school. In his own words, after experiencing the condition, Edeh has this to say:

"Following the devastating Nigerian Civil War, the educational system in the country had almost collapsed, giving way to the reign of secret cultism activities, rampant killings, and destruction of lives and property in and around almost all the tertiary institutions. Students, geared by some members of staff, organize killings of both staff and fellow students. Riots, strikes, and a state of chaos and confusion had almost taken over campuses of tertiary institutions in the country" (Edeh, 2007).

Edeh's presence in the Nigerian educational system has brought great relief to many Nigerian youths and their parents who are sure of their education even without much stress. The quality of education is now assured since there is a corruption-free environment for studies in all Edeh's institutions of learning. Hence, Edeh's role has been that of the saviour of our nation's educational scheme. He is a servant leader who gives himself to suffering for his people. He sets the pace for others to follow and his works of education speak volumes about this educational giant of our time.

Educational Empowerment

Fr Edeh realised that the best empowerment he could give to the teeming youths around him is quality education. At this time, the education system in Nigeria was in a deplorable state and good education could only be acquired overseas. He was of the view that education was not a luxury, but a necessity for every human being for proper development. According to Nwoye, "It is only through quality education that people can unleash the latent talents in them and actualize their potential as well." To achieve this in the lives of these abjectly poor people, Fr Edeh established schools in different levels ranging from nursery and kindergarten schools to universities. Consequently, moved by the conviction that these people are the "good that are," Edeh availed the people living under the Pilgrimage Centre Charity an opportunity to have good and functional education without cost. They are under special scholarship scheme which was put in place by the founder which includes free tuition, food, and accommodation.

It is to the glory of God and for human development that led Edeh to establish the following educational institutions:

1. Elizabeth Nursery and Primary School Akpugo, Enugu State
2. Caritas Nursery, Primary, and Secondary School, Garki, Abuja
3. Madonna International Secondary School, Kuje, Abuja
4. Our Saviour Nursery and Primary School, Elele, River State
5. Our Saviour International Secondary School, Elele, Rivers State
6. Our Saviour Girls Secondary School, Aba, Abia State
7. OSISATECH Boys Secondary School, Emene, Enugu State
8. OSISATECH Girls Secondary School Independence Layout, Enugu State
9. Caritas Secondary School, Ibadan, Uyo State
10. OSISATECH College of Education, Enugu State
11. OSISATECH Polytechnic, Enugu
12. Caritas University Enugu, Enugu State
13. Madonna University Nigeria (with Elele, Okija, and Akpugo Campuses)

Those who are physically challenged are not left out in the educational programme. They are also trained in the manner that their nature can assimilate. The founder had them in mind when he established the Polytechnic and College of Education (OSISATECH Polytechnic and OSISATECH College of Education). Special attention is given to those who are blind, deaf, mute, and physically disabled. Trained professionals are employed in these schools to give them sound and quality education. They are also under the scholarship scheme.

Socio-Economic Empowerment

A man without a means of sustenance, especially in a developing country, could be likened to a ship without a captain in the middle of an ocean being tossed around by wind. Such a person lacks peace in his heart and finds it difficult to live in peace with his neighbours. This is why Fr Edeh did not stop at giving them food alone, but went ahead to teach them how to fend for themselves. Fr Edeh is a man who not only gives you fish to eat but teaches you how to fish. He established for them a rehabilitation centre where they are introduced to self-help projects like the art of making soap, detergent, pomade, sachet water, wine, tissue, paint, printing, and much more. There are testimonies abound that numerous people who pass through this centre are gainfully employed and are fending for themselves. It is interesting to remark that the first group of people who passed through this centre, trained by Fr Edeh himself, have become married men and women living comfortable and fulfilled lives.

4.7. EDEH'S EDUCATION FOR ALL

Education for All (EFA) has been the major priority programme of UNESCO. This had informed different conferences over the years. For instance, the UNESCO's world conferences on education in Jomtian, Thailand, in 1990 and the world education forum in Dakar, Senegal, in 2000 were all in the agreement on Education for All. The implication is the need for equality of education in the world—especially in Africa where gender inequality for education has been very obvious until Edeh's intervention.

Equality of opportunities in all spheres of human endeavours is the priority of Edeh's educational policies. Due to the encounters of the great contradictions between the ideal of equal opportunity (as being propagated by the government and other bodies such as UNESCO) and the existence of the present condition of the educational programme in the country (Nigeria), there was every need for a redeemer. It was a situation where only the rich could afford education, while the majorities that are poor and handicapped had no hope for education. On this note, Kishan (2008, p. 8) holds that the "EFA programme can especially unite the chances for those who have the ability, but do not unfortunately have the required social, economic, or regional advantage."

Edeh's educational system is a conscious effort for the education for all. It therefore became and is still an opportunity for the parents to train their children in a good school with confidence and assurance of their safety and for the children to have the privileges of being accepted in the labour market after graduation. Based on his philosophy, the holistic caring for man cannot be achieved without a working and affordable/formidable educational system. Edeh advocates for the equality of education for all—men and women alike—and focusing on giving the opportunity for education to both the poor, the handicapped, and physically challenged. He has a scholarship scheme where many youths are the beneficiaries.

According to Edeh (2007, p. 90), "The establishment of the above tertiary institutions ushered in reformation for good in the entire educational system in the country—proper, effective, and functional education devoid of secret cultism, riots and strikes, examination malpractice" and many other vices. Edeh has scholarship schemes in these institutions where the abjectly poor and the handicapped are given scholarships. The teeming numbers of youth of our country have been saved from the menace of social and moral vices in our society, thereby giving them the hope of life and responsibilities in the society.

With all these achievements by Fr Edeh in the education sector, which no single person has ever done in Africa, he stands as the pillar of education in Africa and more especially in Nigeria. He has set a pace for both the governments and individuals in Africa to emulate.

Special Features of Edeh's Educational Empowerment

Discussed below are concrete and humane ways in which Fr Edeh is implementing his doctrine and philosophy of Practical and Effective Charity in the context of youth empowerment educationally:

Work-study programme: This enables the youths whose parents or guardians are unable to pay their school fees to work within the institution, receiving their wages which help them to defray the full cost of their education.

Scholarship Scheme for Excellence: This scheme encourages and rewards excellence. Students who have distinguished themselves in any field of endeavour that promotes holistic, human well-being are usually encouraged and rewarded either by a cash prize or some form of scholarship (full or partial). For example, a good number of students are enjoying tuition-free education for academic excellence.

Scholarship for Indigent Youths: Those whose parents are abjectly poor. There are a number of bright youths who desire to further their education but their parents cannot afford the fees because of their social and economic conditions for those on the margins of society. For the beneficiaries of this scheme, it is manna from heaven.

Special Scholarship Programmes for the Physically Challenged: This category of persons is usually further marginalized by societal neglect except in some communities where some individuals take the bull by the horns and do something positively and affirmatively to improve their lot. Emmanuel M. P. Edeh's philosophy and perception of man (in whatever form or shape) as the "good that is" or *mmadi* have compelled and guided his commitment to the growth of people. Fr Edeh is convinced that people have an intrinsic value beyond their contributions as workers. Nothing seems to stop him in his efforts to nurture the personal, spiritual, and professional growth of all he is in relation and association with, especially the downtrodden and on the margins of society. This special scholarship programme is available in all of his institutions, but more so in OSISATECH Polytechnic and College of Education in Ogui, Enugu.

Special Scholarship Programme for Host Communities: The communities in which Fr Edeh's establishments and institutions are sited enjoy special scholarships which are aimed as contribution to community development and enrichment through youth education and empowerment. As a generous leader, Fr Edeh is teaching and encouraging both the youth and communities the art of returning something to or investing something in a society or community from which one has received something. As a charismatic leader, Fr Edeh has a very clear understanding that serving others is important, especially in the values and ideas that shape the society positively and productively.

4.8. ECONOMIC EMPOWERMENT THROUGH THE CREATION OF JOB OPPORTUNITIES

Rehabilitation Centre for the Mentally Deranged

As was noted earlier, after the Nigerian-Biafran civil war, many people were frustrated, abandoned, condemned to live in absolute solitude and loneliness. Some even suffered the effect of charms and the psychological effects of long-standing land disputes. Thus, the effects of these multiple societal problems on people produced a great number of mentally deranged people. These persons are usually brought and abandoned in the Pilgrimage Centre premises by their relatives. Fr Edeh in his humane and compassionate manner, gathers them in a place and caters for them. Some of these cases are serious and violent while others are mild and non-violent, but each of them is given adequate medical attention. They are all placed under the watchful care of specialist doctors and nurses free of charge. After their treatment and their full recovery, they are put in the rehabilitation centre where they can learn work and be gainfully employed.

4.9. EDEH'S EMPLOYED WORKERS CHART (EEWC)

Establishments	Academic/Senior Staff	Non-Academic/ Junior staff	Artisans
Madonna University	485	660	4000
OSISATECH Polytechnic/ College of Education	157 80	187 88	773 1000
Madonna University Teaching Hospital	226	77	2000
Pilgrimage Centre	200	1000	10,000
Catholic Prayer Ministry (CPM)	280	2000	4000
Saviourite House of Formation	43	-	9
Prestigious Madonna Int'l Art and Sci. Sec. Sch. Kuje Abuja	41	48	50
Our Saviour Nursery and Primary Sch., Elele	15	7	-
Our Saviour Int'l Sec. Sch., Elele	22	8	40
Our Saviour Girls Sec. Sch., Aba	29	25	10
OSISATECH Boys Sec. Sch., Enugu	30	8	30

OSISATECH Girls Sec. Sch. Enugu	30	16	-
Elizabeth Model Nursery, Primary & Sec. Sch. Akpugo	21	3	-
Elizabeth Model Schools Area 3, Garki Abuja	44	20	7
Caritas Nursery/Primary and Sec. Sch. Ibadan	24	60	20
Paint Factory	-	50	10
Water Factory	-	17	-
Printing Press	-	48	48
Mayfresh Bank	23	132	1000
Ohha Bank	10	39	600
Triumph Soft Drink			300
Total	1,760	4493	23897
Grand Total	30,150		

4.10. THE UNIQUE NATURE OF EDEH'S ECONOMIC EMPOWERMENT

From the above exposition, it is obvious that Edeh's mode of empowerment is second to none and its uniqueness cannot be overlooked without denying posterity an aspect of the life of this superservant leader which is essential. He is a man who is down-to-earth and self-giving. He lives with abjectly poor people and tries to share in their condition. Living with them helps him to identify their unique talents and tries to help them make proper use of it. He believes that there is a latent power in every individual waiting to be unleashed. Thus, he accompanies them and offers them useful advice.

After undergoing the rehabilitation programme, they are not left to be on their own. Fr Edeh either employs them in one of his establishments or mobilizes them to establish themselves. They are given money to start their own business. This programme is life-giving, in that it flows from his philosophy of man. He believes that man is *mmadi*, "the good that is," since he is a creature of the Supreme Being. He argues that man who shares in the goodness of God ought to be cared for, respected, and loved by his fellow men as a means of maintaining the God-man relationship and man-man relationship (Edeh, 2009, pp. 44, 48).

Another unique aspect of Edeh's empowerment program is that it is charity-based which respects the ontological status of a person. Those undergoing this programme are not expected to pay any money during or after the programme. It is purely an act of charity geared towards alleviating poverty in the world and achieving the goal of world peace.

The charity aspect of this programme has taken a new and fabulous dimension by recognising and appreciating those who have participated in grassroots charity extensively. This is the main contention of the next chapter.

CHAPTER FIVE

MADONNA INTERNATIONAL CHARITY PEACE AWARD

5.1. THE MEANING AND PURPOSE

The Madonna International Charity Peace Award (MICPA) is an award of excellence given to special individuals in recognition of their immense contribution towards alleviating or ameliorating the pain and sufferings of those living in abject poverty in the society. This humanitarian act could be in the form of education, provision of relief materials, housing, food, security, etc. This initiative is the brainchild of Fr Edeh but has a deep rooted history with his biological mother whose influence on Fr Edeh cannot be over-emphasized.

The idea of having such a platform as MICPA through which those who have distinguished themselves in alleviating human suffering are honoured to help reach out to people within and outside the shores of Nigeria and Africa. The reality of suffering is the same everywhere in the world and there are individuals who have done well in ameliorating the situation. Humanity has known the effects of the ignoble experiences of wars, natural disaster, hunger, poor leadership, diseases, and class oppression which have brought destitution in our society. These victims who are in their great numbers are without food, clothing, shelter, money, and education. These people often live only at the mercy of those with charitable hearts who come to provide for them.

MICPA therefore is created to appreciate the effort of those whose primary concern it is to help the destitute. In this way, they are encouraged and empowered to do more. The financial gift to the awardees serves as a re-enforcement which spurs them to undertake more charitable works.

The institution of the Madonna International Charity Peace Award (MICPA) is a veritable channel of pursuing the global course for world peace. It encourages charitable works and care for the destitute, abjectly poor, the marginalized, the abandoned, the sick and the suffering people who are helpless and disillusioned. These categories of people are obviously far from the experience of peace and they constitute the greater number of the world's population. Arguably, a malnourished and sick person cannot be said to be living in peace. Thus, the task of providing these essential needs to them is a way of bringing peace to their hearts which will eventually translate into world peace. Hence, MICPA is a charitable venture that encourages more charitable works from those with the spirit aimed at the rediscovery of world peace.

5.2   THE ORIGIN OF THE MADONNA INTERNATIONAL CHARITY PEACE AWARD

As mentioned in the previous chapter, the mother of Fr Edeh was a woman of profound charity which earned her the name MAMA OMEOGO, meaning 'the Mother of Charity'. She practically gave all that she had at any point in time to aid those in need. Through the practical and effective charity of her mother, Fr Edeh came to the realisation that human suffering is a phenomenon that should be tackled headlong and approached with spirit of sacrifice. Obviously, to put a smile on the faces of those who are suffering, one must be ready to forgo certain pleasures and comfort.

Shortly before she died in February 1996, the mother of Fr Edeh willed all her savings to Edeh (Biodata of a Legend of our Time, 2011, p. 234). She passionately appealed to her son to use the money for charity. The testimonies of today show that he made judicious use of the money. Under the inspiration of the Holy Spirit, Fr Edeh, did not just distribute the money to the poor people, rather he invested the money on a small-scale project with the aim of using the proceeds specifically for the poor. To this day, the project on which the money was invested has continued to yield proceeds which Fr Edeh has not relented in using it for the poor.

Onyewuenyi (2010, P. 81) records that at first, Edeh used the money willed to him by his mother to establish the Umuofo Community Bank which was consequently transformed into Mayfresh Savings and Loans Ltd. It is the annual proceeds of the bank that Fr Edeh uses in carrying out the mission of practical and effective charity. This practice has been in the ministry of Fr Edeh, but the contribution of his mother has helped to make it continuous, stable, and standardized.

On 26 November 2006, Very Rev Fr Emmanuel M.P. Edeh inaugurated the Madonna International Charity Peace Award (MICPA) as a way of respecting the last wish of his mother (Biodata of a Legend of our Time, 2011, P.236). This is to bring the mission of Practical and Effective Charity across borders and to immortalize Mama Omeogo's charity.

Another major factor that has kept this mission of Practical and Effective Charity alive is the Edeh's philosophy of man. In his epochal treatise, Edeh posits that man is good that is following his claim that he is created by a being that is good in se (Edeh, 1985, p.102). Hence, if man is good that is, realities that depict man as such ought to be established to instil peace and tranquillity in his heart.

5.3.   WHO IS ELIGIBLE TO WIN THE AWARD?

Similar to other renowned awards in the world, MICPA is not given to anybody in the street, or to people seeking political recognition or cheap popularity. It follows strict and stringent conditions that must be met before a person is deemed worthy to be conferred with the award. First and foremost, the individual must be a charitable person who possesses the spirit of unconditional love—giving without the intention of receiving. The person must be seriously engaged in grassroots charity aimed at alleviating human suffering and extreme poverty within his/her locality. In other words, his/her own people must be able to give testimonies of his/her charitable deeds. The emphasis is on the alleviation of human suffering. A person is not honoured with the award because he/she is sharing cars to those working in his/her company or because he/she is sharing food to the hungry during his/her political campaign. It must be a regular practice which a person is known for.

Pertinent too, the person must be an advocate and lover of charity. He/she must be someone who understands the power of charity and does encourage other financially well-placed people to do charity. There are reputable individuals who are charged with the responsibility of screening candidates for the award. It is purely based on tested and approved merit.

5.4.   THE JOURNEY SO FAR

The Charity Peace Award has been given to merited individuals on so many occasions. The first of its kind went to Mrs Mary Maduka, the organiser of "Omeogo Charity Home" Makurdi, Benue State, Nigeria, and Most Rev Rene Marie Ehouzou, the Catholic Bishop of Port-Novo, Benin Republic, who runs a charitable home for destitute. On 9 April 2010, this annual event was repeated where cash award of $60,000 US was given to the victims of Haiti earthquake through Archbishop Kelvin Felix. Similarly, $40,000 US went to suffering children of Vietnam and Philippines through Archbishop Fernando Kapalla. The third edition of this historical event which took place in 2011 was remarkable and special because of the award recipients. Four people who excelled in the act of charity were carefully selected from different parts of the world. They include: Leanghoin Hoy, a Buddhist from Cambodia (Asia); a couple, Mr N'JokBibum and Mrs Margaret Bibum who are physically challenged (deaf and mute); Madam Ngo Djob Marie Catherine from Cameroun, and Mr Christopher Ezeaguka. Following the policy of MICPA which is to further the course of generating and promoting peace in the heart of the disadvantaged people in the society, they were rewarded for their works as follows: while Leanghoin Hoy received $40,000, the other three received $20,000 each (Chukwuemeka Nicholas: Edeh's Charity Peace Model (2nd ed.), 2012, p.168-176).

In 2012, the following persons were awarded: The Missionary Sisters of Charity received $40,000 in recognition of the humanitarian work they are doing for the poor people in Calcutta, India. In the same vein, the family of Mr./Mrs. Emmanuel Obiukwu received cash of N200,000, a Jeep, and full scholarship at Madonna University to the two of the children remaining (Maureen and Celestine Obiukwu) after the bomb blast in St. Theresa's Catholic Church, Madalla, Niger State, that killed four of their children.

In 2013, the award went to a couple, Ray and Jill Wagner from England. They own a charity home where abandoned or adopted children are taken care of.

5.5. THE RELEVANCE OF MICPA TO OUR MODERN WORLD

The relevance of such awards as MICPA cannot be overemphasized in our modern world. We are in a world tormented by individualism and greed but bereft of peace. The spirit of unconditional giving and gospel of brotherhood has grown cold while wickedness has taken the centre stage. Philanthropy has become a political strategy for attracting the attention and sympathy of the people. The institution of MICPA is therefore a wake-up call to all and sundry. It is a clarion call that if world-peace must be attained, we must understand the worth of a human person, love and care for him/her. We must learn to better the plight of those who are troubled on every side, and are lacking peace in their hearts.

The modern man is in dire need of peace. We have experienced all manner of tragedies ranging from natural disasters, political instability and tribal and religious conflicts. The fact that Fr Edeh was able to touch human lives across the globe irrespective of culture, tribe, religion, colour, or race is a proof that world peace is realisable. For instance, during the Madonna University Annual International Convention, during which the award is given, thousands of people from different walks of life and different religions and cultures gather in one place for intellectual brainstorming, disregarding their differences.

Fr Edeh emphasizes respect for man as man not as a black or white. Man as man is ontologically good and deserves nothing but care, respect, and love. Through his mission of practical and effective charity, Edeh has brought relief, peace, love, and care to the poorest of the poor (*umuogbenye*), abandoned, lowly, troubled youths and troubled homes by introducing them into self-help project where they can be gainfully employed. If Fr Edeh alone can achieve all these, why can't we achieve more through collective effort? At this stage in human development, it has become safe to think in terms of peace. Huge resources are wasted on daily basis to wage war and human resources are also lost in the process.

The United Nations realised the effects of constant wars, hatred, sickness, hunger and extreme poverty, illiteracy, and initiated a global fight against them under the caption: Millennium Development Goals (MGDs). These goals which are eight in number are geared towards restoring peace in the heart of man. It is needful to state that Fr Edeh's contributions to these areas already predate for more than a decade the commencement of the United Nations MDGs. Before the United Nations declaration in the year 2000 which eventually gave birth to the MDGs, Fr Edeh had been in the vanguard of poverty alleviation and education empowerment since mid 1980s. It is therefore vital that the world should borrow a leaf from his philosophy of man for the realisation of the MDGs.

CHAPTER SIX

RELIGIOUS INSTITUTIONS AS MEANS OF PERPETUATING PEACE

6.1. RELIGION

Etymologically, "religion" is derived from the Latin *religio* which refers to the ultimate origin of which is obscure. One possibility is an interpretation traced to Cicero, connecting *lego* "to read," *lego* also means or has the sense of "to choose," "to go over again" or "to consider carefully." Modern scholars such as Tom Harpur and Joseph Campbell favour the derivation from *ligare* "bind, connect," probably from a prefixed *re-ligare* that is, re (again) and *ligare* or "to reconnect," which was made prominent by St. Augustine, following the interpretation of Lactantius. According to the philologist Max Müller, the root of the English word "religion" from the Latin *religio* was originally used to mean only "reverence for God or the gods, careful pondering of divine things, piety" (Max Müller, "Lectures on the Origin and Growth of Religion," 1878). The word *religion* is sometimes used interchangeably with faith, belief system, or sometimes set of duties; however, in the words of Émile Durkheim, religion differs from private belief in that it is "something eminently social" (Emile Durkheim E., 1915, p. 10).

Edward Burnett Tylor defined religion as "the belief in spiritual beings" (Tylor, E.B., 1871, p. 424). He argued, back in 1871 that narrowing the definition to mean the belief in a supreme deity or judgment after death or idolatry and so on would exclude many people from the category of religious, and thus has the fault of identifying religion, rather with particular developments than with the deeper motive which underlies them. He also argued that the belief in spiritual beings exists in all known societies (Tylor, E.B., 1871, p. 424).

The typical dictionary definition of religion refers to a "belief in, or the worship of, a god or gods" or the "service and worship of God or the supernatural." However, writers and scholars have expanded upon the "belief in god" definitions as insufficient to capture the diversity of religious thought and experience.

The anthropologist Clifford Geertz defined religion as a "system of symbols which acts to establish powerful, pervasive, and long-lasting moods and motivations in men by formulating conceptions of a general order of existence and clothing these conceptions with such an aura of factuality that the moods and motivations seem uniquely realistic" (Geertz, C., 1993, pp. 87-125).

The psychologist William James in his book *The Varieties of Religious Experience*, defined religion as "the feelings, acts, and experiences of individual men in their solitude, so far as they apprehend themselves to stand in relation to whatever they may consider the divine." By the term *divine*, James meant "any object that is godlike, whether it is a concrete deity or not" to which the individual feels impelled to respond with solemnity and gravity (James, W., 1902, pp. 31-38).

It is noteworthy that echoes of James' and Durkheim's definitions are to be found in the writings of Frederick Ferre who defined religion as "one's way of valuing most comprehensively and intensively." Religion could also be regarded as an organized collection of beliefs, cultural systems, and world views that relate humanity to an order of existence. Many religions have narratives, symbols, and sacred histories that are intended to explain the meaning of life and/or to explain the origin of life or the universe. From their beliefs about the cosmos and human nature, people derive morality, ethics, religious laws, or a preferred lifestyle. The practice of a religion may also include rituals, sermons, commemoration or veneration of a deity, gods or goddesses, sacrifices, festivals, feasts, trance, initiations, funeral services, matrimonial services, meditation, prayer, music, art, myth, dance, public service, or other aspects of human culture.

6.2. INSTITUTIONS (CONGREGATIONS)

This term *institution* is commonly applied to customs and behaviour patterns important to a society. An institution is any structure or mechanism of social order governing the behaviour of a set of individuals within a given community. Institutions are identified with a social purpose, transcending individuals, and intentions by mediating the rules that govern living behaviour. Institutionalization may also be used in referring to organization of particular bodies responsible for overseeing or implementing policy, for example in welfare or development. That is simply to say, institutions are not mere buildings or places, but structures of relationship, obligation, role, and function. It is therefore from this background that Douglass North offers the following definition: "Institutions are the rules of the game in a society or, more formally, are the humanly devised constraints that shape human interaction" (Douglass North, 1990, p.3).

The effectiveness and efficiency of organization helps in providing the continuity and success to the enterprise. There are many factors that explain the importance and objectives of organisation and Edeh being aware that an efficient and sound organisation make easy for the management to relate the flow of resource continually to the overall objectives (peace), sets to found religious institutions as agents and promoters of peace in our contemporary world. The term *institution* could be liken to *congregation*. Each congregation is presided over by a superior with a title such as Abbot General, Superior General, Mother General, and so on as the case may be.

The 1917 Code of Canon Law reserved the name *religious order* for institutes in which the vows were solemn, and used the term *religious congregation* or simply *congregation* for those with simple vows. The members of a religious order for men were called *regulars*, those belonging to a religious congregation were simply *religious*, a term that applied also to regulars. For women, those with simple vows were simply *sisters*, with the term *nun* reserved in canon law for those who belonged to an institute of solemn vows, even if in some localities they were allowed to take simple vows instead, this implies therefore that, congregations are institutes.

6.3. EDEH'S RELIGIOUS INSTITUTIONS AS AN AGENT OF PEACE

To underline the importance of promoting understanding, tolerance, and friendship among human beings in all their diversity of religion, belief, culture, and language, Fr Edeh encourages universal respect for and observance of human rights and fundamental freedoms for all humanity based on his philosophy of man as that "good that is" (Edeh, 1985, p.100). Without distinction of race, sex, language, or religion as the distinctive features, African philosophy is conceived in theory and brought to reality through practice, as Edeh submits in his book *Peace to the Modern World*. "African philosophy is the way of life expressed in the people's rituals, language, and other cultural manifestations. This philosophy offers people an ideal of human existence, an ideal of human dignity based upon the ontological good and deserving of care and respect" (Edeh, 2006, p. 1).

In a world threatened by ethnic and religious strife, a widening gap between rich and poor, and violent confrontations over dwindling resources, the need to solve conflicts fairly and non-violently has never been more pressing. Edeh explores the roots of violence in the world, including the violence of racism and economic inequality, the origins and perpetuation of war and terrorism, approaches to non-violent conflict resolution, and various paths to social and economic justice in a bid to providing peace to the world. He concurred that peace is an occurrence of harmony characterized by the lack of violence, conflicting behaviours, and the freedom from fear of violence. Commonly understood as the absence of hostility and retribution, peace also suggests sincere attempts at reconciliation, the existence of healthy or newly healed interpersonal or international relationships, prosperity in matters of social or economic welfare, the establishment of equality, and a working political order that serves the true interests of all.

Edeh maintains that peace cannot last without the establishment of institutions that will constantly and continually promote and create environment of peace. Justice is a condition for peace and it demands respect of all by all and for all; it eschews social and economic inequalities. To this effect, in order to perpetuate his peace philosophy and practical programmes that address many concrete needs of man, Edeh has founded many religious congregation of men and women who by their charism and apostolate are poised to continue to render selfless services to humanity especially to the poor, sick and the suffering.

6.4.   RELIGIOUS INSTITUTIONS

Considering the enormous institutions which God has used Fr Edeh to establish, it became paramount to have religious congregations which will sustain them in the spirit of service and charity.

a.   The Sisters of Jesus the Saviour (SJS)

The Congregation of the Sisters of Jesus the Saviour (SJS) is a religious institute of women in the Catholic Church, whose mission is to perpetuate Fr Edeh's Charism and vision of peace, education, care of the sick, the poor, the handicapped, and the suffering people of God. It is principally the sisters who run the health and social welfare institutions. They are specially in charge of the *umuogbenye* (poorest of the poor), a unit in the Pilgrimage Centre where food is cooked and distributed three times to the inmates who are so abjectly poor that they cannot afford even one meal a day. Some came as little ones abandoned and picked on the streets with no knowledge of their parents or relations. The sisters are also actively involved in education. The Sisters' Institute has got many communities (convents) within and outside Nigeria. Among the convents outside Nigeria are the SJS Communities in Miami, Detroit, and New York all in the USA. Others are in Germany, England, Italy, and Caribbean Islands. Founded in 1984, the sisters are the first religious fruit of the Catholic Prayer Ministry of the Holy Spirit founded by Fr Edeh.

b.   The Fathers of Jesus the Saviour (FJS)

The Congregation of the Fathers of Jesus the Saviour was founded on 21 February 1990. The Congregation of the Fathers of Jesus the Saviour is a religious institute with its own specific apostolate of caring. This apostolate of caring stems from the vision the founder had when he set out to provide care to the troubled world. On the physical level, the congregation endeavours to assist the suffering people of God through material aids. The congregation renders assistance to the suffering in the society, for these people stand out as the physical Christ who comes regularly knocking on our doors, asking for help, whom when the door is opened, enters and pours down blessings upon the house owners.

Another means through which the congregation helps individuals physically is by enrolling the individuals in skills-acquisition establishments. It is aimed at training people who, at the end of their training period, start off their own trade or profession. It is proper to mention here that the congregation has been able to train many young people who are today economically buoyant and themselves employers of labour in different fields of life.

As regards the psychological aspect of the caring apostolate, the congregation armed with her learned clerical members embarks on reinstating the psychological well-being of suffering people. There are members trained to revive the drooping psyche of individuals who have lost hope of survival within this world of misery. In order to rescue psychologically unbalanced victims, the congregation not only refers the victims to the doctors, she also makes sure that the victims are properly attended to by the medics and most times would pay the bills.

Furthermore, the congregation provides conducive environments for the psychologically ill; good shelter and proper feeding services are rendered to them as well. The destitute Centre in the Pilgrimage Centre, Elele, is a typical example of the apostolate of caring of the congregation. Here the poor and the downtrodden are brought together and their feeding, clothing, shelter, and health are superlatively taken care of. In Madonna University Teaching Hospital (MUTH) a super health institution owned by the congregation, meticulous medical attention is constantly given to patients. As a result of this attention, numerous patients have been cured of their previously protracted ailments and have returned to their normal state of health, both of mind and body.

The third caring apostolate which the congregation undertakes is the spiritual well-being of individuals. Here, the congregation has for its source of strength Jesus in the Blessed Sacrament. The members draw strength from Jesus the Saviour through constant adoration of Our Lord Jesus Christ in the Blessed Sacrament. With this, the members are then able to go out to solve the spiritual problems of the people. Apart from solving the people's spiritual problems, the members are able to rescue people from demonic attacks and control.

The social aspect is another part of the caring apostolate which the congregation emphasizes and undertakes. The congregation encourages and fosters social services which are aimed at upgrading the lives of the suffering people of God in the society. The members, through their way of life, influence the people who interact with them and guide them to the practice of fraternal love within the society thereby promoting peace. The congregation also has many communities within the country and across the globe.

c. The Contemplatives of Jesus the Saviour (Male)

Contemplatives of Jesus the Saviour, founded in the year 1992, is a community of religious monks who have taken it upon themselves to spend their entire lives on Earth in solitude praying for peace, Harmony, and love of God among men. They are a hidden spiritual powerhouse for the progress and efficacy of all of Fr Edeh's endeavours and establishments.

d. The Contemplatives of Jesus the Saviour (Female)

The female Contemplatives of Jesus the Saviour was founded in the year 2006. Her members live in their own monastery/nunnery at Emene, Enugu, Nigeria. Like the male contemplatives, these nuns devote themselves to a cloistered life of contemplative prayer.

It is worthy of note that the four religious congregations founded by Fr Edeh share the same charism of which is a clear indication that all were founded to promote peace in the chaotic-troubled world, through their lives to restore the sense of the sacred, which is fast eluding the world today. Through their lives of sacrifice, the members sanctify themselves and thus equip themselves spiritually to sanctify others, thus bringing peace to the modern world.

e. The Catholic Prayer Ministry (CPM)

One of the associations founded by Fr Edeh as means of perpetuating peace in the modern world is the Catholic Prayer Ministry Worldwide. It is an association numbering millions in her membership. Drawn from people of all walks of life, creed and gender, the CPM seeks to carry on Christ's saving message of peace to the world. It follows the footsteps of its founder, Fr Edeh, in its promotion of peace and reconciliation, the care of the sick, oppressed, poor and the downtrodden, irrespective of race, colour, sex, or religion. It was founded in the year 1984. Its zones have been established in several cities in the United States of America, United Kingdom, France, Germany and Austria, Holland, and London.

f. The Pilgrimage Centre of Eucharistic Adoration, Elele, Nigeria

To carry out his peace and reconciliation ministry, Fr Edeh founded the Pilgrimage Centre of Eucharistic Adoration, Elele. It is also referred to as the Pilgrimage Centre of Peace and Reconciliation, where thousands of people with broken hearts come and find peace and reconciliation. Elele which before the coming of Fr Edeh was an obscure and unknown village in the bush, quickly became a household name, a famous town, a very prominent centre of pilgrimage in modern Africa and in fact, the largest pilgrimage centre in Africa and fifth in the world after Rome, Jerusalem, Lourdes, and Portugal. During the monthly pilgrimage week, which occurs in the first week of every month, all roads lead to Elele. The foundation stone of this great centre was blessed by his Holiness Saint Pope John Paul II in 1998 during his visit to Nigeria for the beatification of Fr Tansi.

A very serious question at this juncture could be: how is peace perpetuated by these aforementioned institutions? The above emphasised institutes perpetuate peace first and foremost through the practice of their charism and apostolate. Caring, as the fundamental apostolate of these institutions, has to do with the holistic care of the sick and suffering people of God by the members of the congregations. This apostolate is carried out religiously by the members, thereby effecting positive changes in the lives of the people they care for. As a holistic approach to caring, the apostolate seeks the complete well-being of an individual, for it undertakes the care of the physical, the psychological, the spiritual, the social, and the educational aspects of the individual. In a world where good education has been relegated to the background, these congregations edge out to care for the people in their academic pursuits. Today, due to corruption, many of our country's educational infrastructures have encountered setbacks, thereby producing half-baked graduates who lack the finesse to practice effectively in their disciplines and fields of trade. These congregations from this background embark on the establishment of educational institutions ranging from primary, secondary to tertiary levels as means of promoting peace among the youths who will in turn be ambassadors for peace in the world.

The basic aim for setting up these institutions is not for profit-making, rather it is an attempt to provide academic panacea for the country and across the globe. In order to stress the presence of the apostolate of caring within these institutions, students are often given scholarships and the physically challenged individuals are usually admitted on free basis because of their deprived status. They, through their apostolate of caring, help the people of God whom they encounter to grow as Jesus grew in wisdom, stature, and in favour with God and men (cf. Luke, 2:52). In general, charism denotes any good gift that flows from God's love and care for humans. The word can also mean any of the spiritual graces and qualifications granted to every Christian to perform his or her task in the Church. In the narrowest sense, it is a theological term for the extraordinary graces given to individual Christians for the good of others (http://nashvilledominican.org/Charism /Characteristics of Our Charism).

The charism of a religious congregation refers to the distinct spirit that animates a religious community and gives it a particular character. A charism is part of the permanent heritage of a community, which includes the rule, mission, history, and traditions kept by the religious institute. The charism of a community is such that if all written records were destroyed, it could be re-created through the living testimony of its members. By implication, members promote peace among themselves since *nemo dat quod non habet* (you cannot give that which you don't have). They perpetuate peace by their everyday living, because it is only when we begin to change our immediate worlds around us, if we begin to spread peace and understanding within our friendships and families, that peace will grow beyond us. It will perpetuate beyond our friends and family, beyond their friends and family, and beyond theirs. It is therefore by living peacefully among themselves that they dish out peace to this world which is seriously in need of peace. Peace, for humanity's sake, when it is enhanced and used properly, through it, we can after in the best our humanity has to offer, without which the world cannot survive.

From the foregoing, the rationale behind Edeh's Peace Model is care for humanity and creation generally. That is also why Edeh's Peace Model is anchored on caring for, and seeing the other as the good that is, and teaching his adherents to do the same. Invariably, destroying oneself and the other is simply destroying goodness.

Pin-pointedly, it is right to say that these institutions are devoted to the apostolate of caring for the sick and suffering people of God all over the world. This implies caring with compassion ...especially the handicapped, the abjectly poor and abandoned in all aspects of caring: namely spiritually, physically, psychologically, socially, and educationally (Edeh, 1993, p. 7). These institutions dedicate themselves to support and strengthen the home and family as the nursery of peace. In homes and families, communities, nations, and the world: they commit themselves to resolving or transforming conflicts without using violence, and to prevent them through education and the pursuit of justice. They commit themselves to work towards a reduction in the scandalous economic differences between human groups and other forms of violence and threats to peace, such as waste of resources, extreme poverty, racism, all types of terrorism, lack of caring, corruption, and crime. They are seriously committed in a truly humane education for all, emphasizing education for peace, freedom, and human rights, and religious education to promote openness and tolerance. Their communities of faith have a responsibility to encourage conduct imbued with wisdom, compassion, sharing, charity, solidarity, and love; inspiring one and all to choose the path of freedom and responsibility as they project peace to the modern world.

As long as these institutions are in existence the perpetuation of peace to the modern world is well assured. Hence, Edeh's wisdom in going through untold sufferings to found and establish properly these institutions is great and cannot be measured.

CONCLUSION

Over a decade ago, the United Nations (UN) came up with a global program tagged the Millennium Declaration. This Millennium Declaration addressed the deplorable states of social justice, global economy, peace and human welfare in general. As a result of these, the United Nations set out to confront negative societal ills through the Millennium Development Goals (MDGs). These goals are eight variegated aims it optimistically anticipated to achieve by 2015 which include eradication of extreme poverty and hunger, universal primary education, promotion of gender equality, reduction of child mortality rate, improvement of maternal health, etc. However, this work has shown that Fr Edeh had started executing and pursuing the actualization of these goals fifteen years earlier than United Nations' Millennium Declaration.

The contributions of Fr Edeh's Charity/*Mmadi* Peace Model, literally, cannot be exhausted in this piece. He has been widely acclaimed by very many individuals, significant among whom is Prof. B.I.C. Ijomah who remarked that "between 1985 and 2002 there is an unsurpassed record of over 14 million cases settled, families reunited and peace brought to communities where there are serious conflicts" by Fr Edeh via his Reconciliation Centre.

The enviable success recorded by Edeh's Peace Model is corroborated in the fact that it is based on the ontological concept of man (all humans) as *mmadi*, the good that is, it is not just a post-conflict peace model in the sense that it is only viable in reconciling parties after the conflict might have ensued. It is both post-conflict and pre-conflict peace model. This is because it starts at the grassroots to reset the mind set of every individual as *mmadi* even before any conflict is envisaged; it is equally viable in reconciliation where there is already an existing tension between parties. It is against this backdrop that Edeh's Peace Model bridges the gap between the strong and the weak, the lion and the lamb, the rich and the poor. It equally tackles the problem of peace from every possible angle both spiritual and material, and by that fact takes the lead among all other existing philanthropic and social peace models.

The international community in its sincere pursuit of this most sought world bride (peace), should incorporate and encourage Edeh's Peace Model. This will go a long way to facilitate and challenge other persons of similar strength to channel it to the realization of this urgent need of the human species. Edeh's Charity/*Mmadi* Peace Model should be appreciated and upheld by both national and international communities as supreme in the practical realization of world peace.

In spite of all efforts being made over the years for peace, human community has experienced springs of violence, insurgency, terrorism and wars that dehumanize man, reducing him from his state of *mmadi* (good that is), and putting him under the burden of suffering, depression, and despair. Some persons of exceptional level of ingenuity have strenuously laboured to bring about peace to the human family. In their labours, many, by their very lives and human dignifying works stand as models of peace. Others by their theory, development of operational principles and policies have developed peace models that are ways of attaining peace. Prominent among the peace models developed by these people are: Mahatma Gandhi's Peace Model, Nelson Mandela's Peace Model, Desmond Tutu's Peace Model, Steve Covey's Peace Model and Edeh's Charity/*Mmadi* Peace Model.

From the cradle of his mission, Edeh developed a Peace Model envisioned to posses the global capacity of restoring the much sorted world peace, a Peace Model that is unique and prevailing founded on the basis of his philosophy of "*mmadi*." man is "good that is" in the sense that having been created by God, he is a product of his maker and hence shares in the being of his maker, the highest good. When one is reoriented to the ontological reality that all men are "goods that are" as they are created and cared for by God one cannot but be at peace with one another, the fellow good that is.

A proper understanding of this philosophy should quench every urge for conflict and strife in every rational human being. *Mmadi* Peace Model is seen under the auspices of charity which is holistic and all-encompassing, that is, Practical and Effective Charity. This charity demands that in serious consideration of the sick, the dying, the suffering, the lonely, the abjectly poor and abandoned, one will not only allow peace to reign, but must foster peace in the hearts of the society. Hence, charity in Edeh's Peace Model has both pre-conflict and post-conflict relevance. For Edeh the dictum that when violence is matched with violence, the man of violence learns the language of peace is changed to when violence is matched with practical and effective charity, the man of violence learns and propagates the culture of peace.

Charity is love and if charity is love and God is love, and then it is correct to say that Edeh's Charity/*Mmadi* Peace Model is God's Peace Model, a peace model God offers to humanity, the totality of *mmadi* through the instrumentality of Fr Edeh through which a lasting peace must return to the world.

As we have seen in this research, Edeh has erected numerous structures and initiatives with enormous strength of instilling tranquillity and calming the intra-personal tension pervading the being of persons. These structures and initiatives are capable of addressing both the spiritual and material worries of millions of people in order to restore their inner tranquillity and peace. With his philosophy which constitutes his Peace Model *Mmadi*, Edeh has succeeded in creating authentic human existence that entails bringing care and supports wholeheartedly to man especially the sick, the suffering the abjectly poor and the abandoned. He has demonstrated the practical applicability of this philosophy by establishing institutions where this love and charity are exhibited to a fault.

Prominent among these institutions is a gigantic Pilgrimage Centre located at Elele, in Rivers State of Nigeria, a centre where millions of people from across the globe gather, both as individuals and groups to find peace in their hearts, lives and families. The Pilgrimage Centre has spread its tentacles with its spiritual and reconciliation activities going on in other countries like England (London, Liverpool, Manchester),

Germany (Essen, Frankfurt, Aachen) America (Miami, Atlanta, Chicago, New York, New Orleans, New Jersey, Austin Texas, Dallas, Washington, California, Boston, Houston), Holland (Den Hague, Amsterdam, Gratz), Austria (Vienna), Caribbean Islands and Italy (Rome, Netturno).

As we have seen Edeh's peace creating institutions in Nigeria also include Centre for Peace, Justice, and Reconciliation, Museum of Charms and Fetish Objects, the educational institutions of all types through which millions of youths are being empowered to fulfill their purpose of existence in life and hence have peace in abundance. His medical institutions, skill acquisition establishments, centres, and projects are all geared towards empowering millions of human beings, the goods that are, to live their God given lives in peace.

Edeh's tremendous efforts towards world peace are infinitely highlighted and perfected through the following activities and programs: The Achievement of Millennium Development Goals, development and implementation of Super Servant Leadership Model, Edeh's Charity/ *Mmadi* Peace Model, Madonna International Charity Peace Award (MICPA). The foundation of four religious congregations all are for assured continuity and perpetuation of the achievement of world peace. It is abundantly obvious that with the philosophy EPTAism spreading round the world and judging from the wonderful effects of the works of this one man the greatly desired world peace is becoming a reality.

BIBLIOGRAPHY

About Stephen R. Covey, https://www.stephencovey.com/about.hph.

Adigwe Zulu: *A Biography of Very Rev Fr Prof. Emmanuel M. P. Edeh C.S.Sp, OFR;* Madonna University Press, Enugu Nigeria, 2011.

Amah, P., (2012), *Emmanuel Edeh: Inspiring 21st Century Africans to Serve First,* Enugu, Nigeria: Madonna University Press, 2012.

Angeles P., Dictionary of Philosophy (N.Y Harper &Row, Publishing, 1981.

Ayer, A. J. *Language, Truth and Logic,* (Victor Gollantz, 1936).

Blum, Paul Richard, *Philosophy and Religion in the Renaissance,* Surrey, England: Ashgate Publishing Limited, 2010.

Catechism of the Catholic Church (CCC), with Modifications from the Editio Typica, Doubleday, 1995.

Carnap Rudolf, *The Logical Structure of the World,* (California: University of California Press, 1967)

Chinua Achebe, *There was a Country,* Penguin Books, USA, 2012.

Chris Trueman, "League of Nations" 2013

Chukwuemeka Nicholas: *Edeh's Charity Peace Model (2nd ed.)* Madonna University Press. Enugu, 2012.

Constitution of the Federal Republic of Nigeria, 1999, Chapter Two, Section 17b.

Daniel J. Sullivan, *An Introduction to Philosophy*, USA, TAN Books, 2012)

Darton Longman et al, eds., Standard Edition, The New Jerusalem Bible. London: Dell Pub.Group Inc., 1985.

Desmond, Tutu, *No Future without Forgiveness*, New York, Doubleday, 1999.

Edeh E. (ed), *The Church of Jesus the Saviour in Africa*, Vol. 2, Enugu, Madonna University Press, 2009.

Edeh E.M.P; *Towards an Igbo Metaphysics*, Loyola University Press, Chicago, America, 1985.

Edeh E.M.P.; *Peace to the Modern World: A Way Forward through the Concrete Living of the Existential Dictates of the African Philosophy of Being*, Minuteman Press, Banbury, United Kingdom, 2006.

Edeh E.M.P; *Igbo Metaphysics: The First Articulation of African Philosophy of Being*, Our Saviour Press, Enugu, Nigeria, 2009.

Edeh, E.M.P., Vol. II, (ed.), *The Church of Jesus the Saviour in Africa*, Nigeria, Madonna University Press Ltd., 2009.

Edeh E.M.P, *The Constitution of the Fathers of Jesus the Saviour, First Edition*, Enugu, Our Saviour Press, 1993.

Edeh E.M.P; *The Constitution of the Sisters of Jesus the Saviour*, Fourth Edition, Enugu, Our Saviour Press, 2007.

Edeh, E. (ed), Jesus *the Saviour in Our Midst Vol. One*, High Wycombe, Catholic Prayer Ministry of the Holy Spirit, 1988.

Emile Durkheim E., *The Elementary Forms of the Religious Life*, London, George Allen & Unwin, 1915.

Enuga S. Reddy, http://www.muthalnaidoo.co.za/indian-south-african-history-enuga-reddy/341-mahatma-gandhi south-africa-and-satyagraha.

Ezechi C., *Actualization of the Millennium Development Goals: Fr Edeh as a Pacesetter*, Madonna University Press, Enugu, Nigeria, 2013.

Ezechi C., *Aspects of Edeh's Philosophy, Vol. Two*, Enugu, Madonna University Press, 2009.

Ezenwajiaku Josephat, *Biodata of a Legend of our Time: Very Rev Fr Prof. Emmanuel Matthew Paul Edeh C.S.Sp, OFR*; Madonna University Press, Enugu, Nigeria, 2011.

Flannery, A., ed, (2001), Vatican Council II, the Conciliar and Post-Conciliar Documents, Mumbai, St. Pauls.

Frederick Ferré, F., *Basic Modern Philosophy of Religion*, Scribner, 1967.

Gandhi, M. K., *The Collected Works of Mahatma Gandhi*, New Delhi, Publication Division, Ministry of Information and Broadcasting, Government of India, 1958-1984.

Geertz, C., *Religion as a Cultural System*, The interpretation of cultures: selected essays, Clifford: Fontana Press, 1993.

Gutek, Gerald L., "History of Education," Microsoft Encarta 2009. Redmond, WA, Microsoft Corporation, 2008).

Harper, Douglas. "Religion." Online Etymology Dictionary.

Hawley Katherine, *Science as a Guide to Metaphysics*, Netherlands, Springer, 2006)

Hume, David, *An Enquiry Concerning Human Understanding*, 1748, 132.

Hobbes, Thomas: "Leviathan" in Molesworth, English Works of Hobbes

Iroegbu, Pantaleon P., *Metaphysics: The Kpim of Philosophy*, Owerri, International Universities Press, Ltd., 1995)

James, W., *The Varieties of Religious Experience. A Study in Human Nature*. Longmans, Green, and Co., 1902.

Jean Jacques Rousseau's *Educational Theories*, extracted from Emilie Julia, USA: Barnous's Educational Services Inc. 1964.

Journal of School of Education Federal College of Education, Eha-Amufu, Vol.1, No. 2.

Karl Marx and Engels, *The Communist Manifesto* in Selected Works, London, Lawrence and Wishart, 1962

Keylor, William R., "World War I," Microsoft Encarta 2009 [DVD], Redmond, WA, Microsoft Corporation, 2008.

Koyré, Alexandre, Metaphysics and Measurement, London, Harvard University Press, 1968.

Kurien Kunnumpuram ed., *World Peace: An Impossible Dream?*, Mumbai, Better Yourself Books, 58/23rd Road, TSP III, 2011.

Lakatos, Imre, "Science: Reason or Religion." Section 1 of "Falsification and the Methodology of Scientific Research Programs" in Imre Lakatos & Alan Musgrave, Criticism and the Growth of Knowledge, Cambridge University Press, 1970.

Ndubaku, P., (2012) Oral Interview with Chief Sir Patrick Ndubaku, over forty years of age, a man who has been an active member of the Reconciliation Centre since 1985.

Madonna International Journal vol. 3, No. 1, May 2010.

Mahatma, Gandhi, An Autobiography, Ahmedabad, 2008.

Marthalev, Bernard (ed.), New Catholic Encyclopedia, second edition, *America: The Catholic University of America*, 2003.

Meredith Martin, *Mandela: A Biography*, UK, Simon & Schuster Ltd., 2010.

Multidisciplinary Journal of Research Development, Vol. 8, Oral Tradition No.1, July, 2007.

Nader El-Bizri,, 'Avicenna and Essentialism' Review of Metaphysics, 2001.

Obi, A.C., (2002), "Senses of Being in Igbo Metaphysics," in Ogunmodede (ed),, West African Journal of Philosophical Studies (WAJOPS), Vol. 5.

Ogbodo, A. U., *A Short Profile of Very Rev Fr Prof.*, 2010.

Okafor, F., *Philosophy of Education and Third World Perspectives*, 2006.

Omoregbe, Joseph I., *Metaphysics Without Tears: A Systematic and Historical Study*, Lagos, Joja Educational Research and Publishers Ltd, 1996.

Onyewuenyi, Remy, *Very Rev Fr Prof. Emmanuel M.P. Edeh: Life and Works*, Madonna University Press, Enugu, 2010.

Onyewuenyi, R., *The Mustard Seed of Jesus the Saviour*, Elele, Enugu, Nigeria, Madonna University Press, 2009.

Oyvind, Tonnesson, *Mahatma Gandhi, the Missing Laureate,*

http://www.nobelprize.org/nobel_prize/themes/peace/gandhi/.

Peace Around the World, http://www.paul.ypteam.com/nelsonmandela.php.

Pope John Paul II, *Post-Synodal Apostolic Exhortation on Reconciliation and Penance in the Mission of the Church Today to the Bishops, Clergy and Faithful*, Rome, 1984.

Prior, Robin, *The First World War*, London: Cassell, ISBN 0-304-35256-X, 1999.

Stephen, R. Covey, *The 3rd Alternative: Solving Life's Most Difficult Problems*, India, New Delhi, Simon & Schuster, 2011.

Ruth, W., Grant & Nathan, T. (ed.), *Some Thoughts Concerning Education of the Conduct of the Understanding* (by Locke, J.), India, Hachett Publishing, Inc., 1996.

Stephen Covey's Model of Peace, http://www.com.ng/stephen.

Stumpf and Fieser, *History and Problems of Philosophy*, 6th Edition, McGraw, Hill Higher Education, 2003.

Tahtinen, U., *Ahimsa: Non-Violence in Indian Tradition*, London: Rider, 1976.

Taylor, Alan John Percivale, *The First World War: An Illustrated History*, Hamish Hamilton, ISBN 0-399-50260-2,OCLC 2054370, 1963.

Tillich, P., *Theology of Culture*, United Kingdom, Oxford University Press, 1959.

Tylor, E.B., *Primitive Culture: Researches Into the Development of Mythology, Philosophy, Religion, Art, and Custom. Vol. 1*, London, 1871.

Ugwu, B., Class Discussion with Bonaventure Ikenna Ugwu, CSSp, Ph.D, a Senior Lecturer at the Spiritan International School of Theology, SIST, Attakwu, Enugu, 9 November, 2009.

Ugwu, B., *The Holy Spirit as Present and Active in Cosmic Turmoil and Human Suffering*: A Dialogue between Pierre Teilhard de Chardin and Jurgen Moltmann, Rome, Pontifical Gregorian University, 2004.

Whiticker, Alan J., *Speeches That Changed the World*, Mumbai, Jaico Publishing House, 2012.

Whitney, W. D., *Roots, Verb-forms, and Primary Derivatives of the Sanskrit Language: A Supplement to His Sanskrit Grammar*, Bibliothek indogermanischer Grammatiken, Leipzig, Breitkopf abd Hartel, London, 1885.

Williams, Paul, et al., *Buddhist Thought: A Complete Introduction to the Indian Tradition*, Routledge, 2000.

Wilhelm, Joseph, (1908), "Charismata." The Catholic Encyclopedia III, Robert Appleton Company, Retrieved 6 July 2010.

Wittgenstein, Ludwig, "Tractatus Logico-Philosophicus." Major Works: Selected Philosophical Writings, Harper Perennial Modern Classics, 2009.

Ziemke, Earl F., "World War II," Microsoft Encarta 2009 [DVD].

Redmond, WA, Microsoft Corporation, 2008.

http://www.etymline.com/index.php/tremeducat, Retrieved 20 February 2014.

William G., New York Times, 2001, June 29 Stanford Encyclopedia of Philosophy, Retrieved 7 March, 2014.

"Homa," Microsoft Encarta 2009, Redmond, WA: Microsoft Corporation, 2008.

Wikipedia.org/wiki/John_Amos_Comeniu, Retrieved 9 March 2014.

http://digital.library.upenn.edu/women/Montessori/method/method.html, Retrieved 12 March 2014.

http://www.geocities.ws/educationalphilosophyari/, Robert Guisepi, Retrieved 14 March, 2014.

http://en.wikipedia.org/wiki/Nelson-Mandela

http://www.historylearningsite.co.uk/leagueofnations.htm, accessed 4 March 2014.

ChrisTrueman, "United Nations," 2013.

http://www.historylearningsite.co.uk/leagueofnations.htm, accessed 4 March 2014.

http://en.wikipedia.org/wiki/metaphysics

Printed in the United States
By Bookmasters